Historical Association Studies

From Luddism to the First Reform Bill
Reform in England 1810–1832

Historical Association Studies

General Editors: Roger Mettam and James Shields

Decolonization
The Fall of the European Empires
M. E. Chamberlain

Gandhi
Antony Copley

British Radicalism and the French Revolution
1789–1815
H. T. Dickinson

From Luddism to the First Reform Bill
Reform in England 1810–1832
J. R. Dinwiddy

Radicalism in the English Revolution 1640–1660
F. D. Dow

Politics in the Reign of Charles II
K. H. D. Haley

Occupied France
Collaboration and Resistance 1940–1944
H. R. Kedward

Britain's Decline
Alan Sked

Bismarck
Bruce Waller

From Luddism to the First Reform Bill

Reform in England 1810–1832

J. R. DINWIDDY

Basil Blackwell

© J. R. Dinwiddy 1986

First published 1986
First published in USA 1987

Basil Blackwell Ltd
108 Cowley Road, Oxford OX4 1JF, UK

Basil Blackwell Inc.
432 Park Avenue South, Suite 1503,
New York, NY 10016, USA

British Library Cataloguing in Publication Data

Dinwiddy, J. R.
From Luddism to the first Reform Bill :
reform in England, 1810–1832. ——(Historical
Association Studies)
1. Social movements —— England —— History
—— 19th century   2. England —— Social
conditions —— 19th century
I. Title   II. Series
303.4'84   HN 385

ISBN   0–631–13952–4

Library of Congress Cataloging in Publication Data

Dinwiddy, J. R. (John Rowland), 1939–
From Luddism to the first Reform Bill.

(Historical Association studies)
Includes index.
1. Great Britain —— Policies and government ——
1800–1837. 2. Great Britain —— Social conditions ——
19th century. 3. Great Britain. Parliament —— Reform.
4. Luddites. I. Title. II. Series.
DA535.D49   1986   941.07   86–13983
ISBN 0–631–13952–4 (pbk.)

Typeset by Photo-graphics, Honiton, Devon

Contents

Preface   vii
1 Whig and Middle-Class Reformism c. 1810–29   1
2 Popular Radicalism c.1810–29   19
3 The Reform Bill Crisis 1829–32   45
4 The Aftermath of Reform   68
References and Further Reading   81
Index   86

Preface

This book examines the reform movements of 1810–32 both in relation to the ideas that inspired them or were used by them, and in relation to the social interests and motives that lay behind them. The main focus is on movements for political or parliamentary reform, but as these cannot be understood in isolation some attention is also paid to other movements of the period such as trade unionism and co-operative socialism. The book is not concerned exclusively with any particular social class; it examines reformism at upper- and middle-class levels as well as working-class radicalism, for here again it is difficult to understand one strand in isolation from others. There are several questions which the book tries to elucidate. What groups of people were seeking political reform, and what programmes did they respectively advocate? What were their reasons for seeking these reforms? And what arguments and other methods did they use in trying to secure their implementation? There are also some related areas which the book does *not* attempt to cover, because for practical purposes in a work of this length lines have to be drawn somewhere. It concentrates on English reform movements, and little is said except incidentally about other parts of the British Isles. It does not analyse conservative responses to pressure for reform, except where it is necessary to say something about these in order to explain the arguments and conduct of the reformers. Nor does it deal extensively with the problem, about which there has been much controversy in recent years, of how far class formation and class consciousness developed in the early nineteenth century, a problem which turns to a considerable extent on the prior question of what criteria for defining and recognizing class are regarded as appropriate. There is a useful survey of this historiographical debate up until the late 1970s by R. J. Morris (1979). The terms 'middle classes' and 'working classes' are used in this book in the rather loose way in which contemporaries used them, with the middle classes covering a very broad social range from wealthy merchants and professional men down to shopkeepers, and with a fuzzy area between middle and working classes at the level of petty tradesmen and working masters. It should also be noted that the term 'universal suffrage' is used, as it was in the early nineteenth century, to signify what should properly have been called 'manhood suffrage'.

J. R. Dinwiddy

1 Whig and Middle-Class Reformism c.1810–29

For most of the period between 1812, when Lord Liverpool's long ministry began, and 1846, when the Conservative party split over the repeal of the Corn Laws, there was a basic division in the Commons between the ministerial side of the House and the Opposition. Of the earlier part of this period, it could hardly be said that a 'two-party' system existed, because a large number of those who customarily supported Liverpool's government did not regard themselves as party men, and there were in addition a number of 'waverers' who sometimes voted with government and sometimes with the Opposition. The Foxite Whigs, however, during their long period in opposition in the 1810s and 1820s, did maintain a large degree of coherence and continuity as a party, though their morale fluctuated and it was sometimes difficult to see what held them together except an almost religious devotion to the memory of Charles James Fox. The party was a somewhat uneasy combination of aristocrats and professional men. The former, who between them controlled a considerable number of seats in the House of Commons as well as possessing great wealth and social prestige, tended to call the tune. For many of them, adhesion to the Whig party was largely a matter of tradition. Their families, they believed, had long been engaged in a patriotic struggle (in which 1688 was the greatest landmark) to protect the liberties of the nation and the balance of the mixed constitution against the encroachments of the executive and the threat of arbitrary government. During George III's reign, the constitutional balance seemed to have tipped dangerously in favour of the executive. A series of episodes – notably in 1766, 1783 and 1807, when largely Whig ministries had been removed from office by the will of the monarch rather than by defeat in the House of Commons – had shown, in their opinion, that the confidence of the Court was more important than that of parliament. Their antagonistic attitude towards the Court might conceivably have been modified if the Prince of Wales, who had been associated with the Foxites for many years, had installed them in office when he became Regent in 1811–12; but in fact he left the ministry in Pittite hands and soon became thoroughly estranged from the Whigs.

The men of ability from non-aristocratic backgrounds who became associated with the aristocratic Whigs in the early nineteenth century adopted the latter's version of constitutional history. But they also drew on a different current of what can (though anachronistically) be called liberal ideas, and they helped to merge this current with the older tradition. It derived to a large extent from the continental and Scottish Enlightenments. Samuel Romilly, Whig Solicitor-General 1806–7, had met Diderot and worked for Mirabeau in the Paris of the 1780s. Henry Brougham and others who were involved in launching the *Edinburgh Review* in 1802, and who subsequently became prominent Whig publicists, had been educated at Edinburgh University, where they had studied a much more varied and modern curriculum – including jurisprudence, political economy and politics – than was available at the two English universities. Such men had an awareness of the economic and social changes and the broad movements of opinion that were occurring in western Europe, and it was as much in this framework as in the narrower one of Britain's constitutional development that their conceptions of liberty and progress were formed. However, while they were very conscious of the growing importance of the 'middling rank' and of its role in social improvement, they were not democrats. In the aftermath of the popular excesses of the French Revolution, they believed in gradual rather than drastic change; and they saw a reasonable prospect of satisfying their own personal ambitions within the existing political structure. It suited them, therefore, to become the auxiliaries of a set of aristocratic families which could be represented as having, in J. G. Lambton's words, a 'hereditary love of freedom', and they were happy to take up and elaborate Whig ideas about the virtues of the balanced constitution. (Thomas, 1979, pp. 46–57; Kriegel, 1980, p. 255.)

To what extent could the Whig party of the early nineteenth century be regarded as a party of reform? In view of the fact that it was an opposition party with the Court firmly against it, and in view of its ingrained suspicion of executive power, it is not surprising that the kind of political reform most favoured by the Whig party was the kind aimed at reducing the 'influence of the Crown' over parliament. As the Rockinghamite Whigs had in the 1770s and 1780s, the Foxites sought a reduction of the patronage which the king's ministers could distribute with a view to strengthening their following in the House of Commons. The Whigs could not deny that since the early part of George III's reign the 'direct' influence of the Crown, as measured by the number of office-holders who had seats in the House of Commons, had been considerably reduced as a result of a process of 'economical' or administrative reform which had been initiated by Rockingham's ministry of 1782 and had then been carried further by the younger Pitt. The Whigs maintained, however, that the 'indirect' influence of the Crown had greatly increased through the growth of civil and military establishments during the war; and they argued further that the increase in the amount of patronage which the government had to dispose of in the country at large did contribute to ministerial strength in parliament, as it was the practice for such patronage to be distributed through (or on the recommendation of) MPs who were friendly to the administration. This meant, it was alleged, that MPs who wanted access to such patronage in order to gratify their connections and constituents had an interest in supporting the government of the day, and voters had an interest in electing government supporters. The Whigs went so far as to claim that the augmented influence of the Crown was the decisive factor in keeping them out of office. Henry Brougham asked rhetorically in the *Edinburgh Review* in April 1810, after the Commons had in effect exonerated the ministry for the mismanagement of the Walcheren expedition: '*If* the influence of government really has *not* increased, how can those things be explained which are daily before our eyes? ... How else account for the continuance of such a ministry as now rules the country?' Similar arguments were being used as late as 1822, when Brougham moved a resolution in the Commons that the influence of the Crown was 'destructive of the independence of parliament'. However, whatever plausibility such arguments might have had at a time of swollen wartime establishments, they were rapidly losing their force in the post-war period. Liverpool's government was being strongly pressed, not only by the Whigs and by radicals or 'economaniacs' such as Joseph Hume, but also by the country gentlemen on whom it relied for much of its parliamentary support, to reduce public expenditure and the level of taxation. The government did commit itself to a number of 'economical' reforms, including, for example, an official decision to phase out sinecure offices; and Lord Londonderry (formerly Castlereagh) was able to announce in the debate on Brougham's motion that over 2,000 posts in the public departments had been suppressed since 1815. 'Old Corruption' was not by any means dead by the 1820s: as William Rubinstein has emphasized (1983), many office-holders continued to receive salaries and fees grossly in excess of their rational desserts, and some remarkable examples of official pluralism survived. None the less, the concessions of the Liverpool government took most of the wind out of Whig sails, and Brougham's motion was the last of its kind. (Dinwiddy, 1985.)

The Whigs – those of them, at least, who were keen to mount a serious challenge to the government – had to look for other issues on which they could differentiate themselves from the Pittites and appeal for public favour. Some of them were anxious to supplement the traditional county influence of the Whig land-owning families by attracting more support from liberal middle-class elements, especially in the towns. The ambitious Brougham, for example, was continually casting around for policies which would give the party a progressive image. At the end of the war he was suggesting that it should take up matters such as tithes, impressment, the poor law, the cost of legal proceedings and the education of the poor in order to improve its standing with the public. During the second and third decades of the century, individual Whigs such as Brougham himself, Sir Samuel Romilly, Sir James Mackintosh and H. G. Bennet *were* responsible for some important initiatives in the fields of legal and social reform. Yet it is doubtful how much the party gained in popularity as a result, for only a handful of Whigs showed an interest in these questions, and such an interest was not by any means a Whig preserve, as is clear from the reforms of the criminal law which Peel effected while he was Home Secretary. One reform which the Whig party as a whole favoured was Catholic Emancipation. But on this matter – as had been shown at the general election of 1807, when the Catholic question was a major issue – the English public was markedly less liberal than the Whigs. Also, of course, the Whigs lost this bond of union in 1829 when the measure was carried, under the pressure of events in Ireland, by Wellington and Peel.

Eventually, in 1830–1, the Whigs were to find another issue of importance on which they could unitedly campaign, and one this time on which they could rally large-scale public support. But for many years previously this issue – parliamentary reform – had been a major source of dissension within the party. In the 1790s it had been one of the main causes of the party split which occurred when the more conservative Whigs headed by the Duke of Portland coalesced with Pitt's government, while those who followed Fox and were more sympathetic to peace and reform remained in opposition. Subsequently, during and after the short-lived coalition ministry of 1806–7 in which the Foxites participated, the issue was a potentially troublesome one because they were then in alliance with the Grenville faction, which was definitely hostile to parliamentary reform; and even among the Foxites themselves there were some influential figures, such as Earl Fitzwilliam, who shared this hostility. A number of Whigs felt much happier about defending civil and religious liberties than about pressing for an extension of political liberty, in the sense of an increased degree of popular control over the political system. Some, like Fox's nephew, Lord Holland, thought that in so far as parliamentary reform was desirable, it was as a means of strengthening the House of Commons against the executive rather than as a means of giving more power to public opinion. Earl Grey, the leader of the party, had introduced motions for reform in the 1790s, but by 1810 had become distinctly luke-warm about it, though he still regarded himself as committed to it in principle.

However, there was another group which believed that the party should take a more positive line over the issue. This point of view was expressed by Francis Jeffrey, editor of the *Edinburgh Review*, in an article of January 1810. Around that time there was a notable revival of public interest in reform, after a decade or more in which the question had been little discussed, and a new group of radicals (or 'patriots', as they were then called) had emerged under the leadership of Sir Francis Burdett. Jeffrey maintained that a dangerous confrontation was building up between the 'courtiers' and the democrats, while the 'constitutional Whigs' in between were becoming increasingly isolated and powerless. What the latter should do, he said, in the interests both of the nation and of themselves, was to ally themselves with the more respectable members of the popular party, in order 'to temper its violence and moderate its excesses, till it can be guided in safety to the defence, and not to the destruction of our liberties'. This strategy would prevent an outright conflict between court and populace, and would recover for the Whigs the extra-parliamentary support which they had been losing through their aloofness and their unwillingness to compete with demagogues for the favour of the people. The policies which they sought to espouse, for the sake of restoring public confidence both in the Whig party and in the constitution, were measures of retrenchment (including the abolition of sinecures) and a moderate reform of the electoral system, including the disfranchisement of rotten boroughs and an extension of the suffrage to respectable classes of citizens who did not yet possess it. In essence, the strategy Jeffrey was advocating was not very different from the one which was to be adopted by the Whigs in 1830. But in 1810 the domestic situation did not, to most people, seem as critical as he made out, and public pressure for parliamentary reform was not great enough to induce the Whig leaders to grasp this nettle. A small number of 'advanced' Whigs who followed the lead of Samuel Whitbread did show a more than nominal support for the cause, and Thomas Brand introduced motions on the subject in 1810 and 1812. But John Allen, confidant of Lord Holland, was stating a view that was more common in Whig circles when he wrote about parliamentary reform in 1810: 'When the country is decidedly for it, the object is so great that it might be worth while to break up the party to obtain it – but to take it up prematurely would divide opposition without advancing the cause of reform.' (British Library of Political and Economic Science, Horner MSS, Allen to Francis Horner, 4 January 1810.)

In the post-war years, the cause did come to be supported by larger numbers of people than ever before. Robert Waithman, the linen draper and City politician who belonged to the radical fringe of the Whig party, wanted men such as Grey and Holland to put themselves at the head of the renascent reform movement. If they did so, he told them, the people would cease to follow visionaries and adventurers, and although the Whigs might lose a few votes in parliament they would be more than compensated by the affection and support of the nation at large. However, although in 1817 the Grenvilles broke away from them and began moving towards an alliance with the government, the Foxite Whigs remained disunited over the reform question; and many of them, disgusted by the extreme and militant nature of the agitation and by what they saw as the disreputable and irresponsible character of its leaders, reacted by dissociating themselves from it and adopting a pessimistic tone about the prospects of reform.

In December of the following year Sir James Mackintosh, lawyer and Whig MP, wrote an article for the *Edinburgh Review* which was one of the fullest and most interesting statements of the case against radical reform. His most basic point was that a variegated suffrage was preferable to a uniform one. A uniform franchise could take the form either of a property qualification or of universal (manhood) suffrage. A uniform property qualification would exclude all those below the level fixed upon and would thus remove the vote from those sections of the lower classes which currently possessed it. Some degree of direct popular representation was highly desirable. Mackintosh said: it provided the common people with a safeguard against oppression, and the admission of some of them to the suffrage gave a sense of participation and self-respect to the lower classes in general. If a broad line of demarcation was drawn between electors and non-electors, the latter would feel excluded and degraded and might be provoked into a dangerous animosity against the system. However, the most mischievous type of uniform suffrage, in Mackintosh's view, would be universal suffrage. His main argument against it was that it would be liable to produce a tyranny of the majority. Such a tyranny was most likely to develop, he said, in a society which was 'divided, by conspicuous marks, into a permanent majority and minority'. He gave as primary examples societies in which there were deep religious or racial divisions; but he added that in almost every country the labouring classes formed a perpetual majority, and that if representation were proportional to numbers no other class would have any real security for its interests. The great strength of the existing system in England, he maintained, was the variety of suffrages which had come into being over the centuries; this heterogeneous franchise made possible 'a union of the principles of property and popularity' and provided representation for all the separate interests of which the general interest was composed. Mackintosh also said in this article that it was beneficial for a representative body to contain a preponderance of landowners: men whose property, education, leisure and 'temperate character' rendered them 'impartial on more subjects than any other class of men'; and he argued for open rather than secret voting on the grounds that the latter would take the animation out of parliamentary elections and would lead to public apathy.

On the face of it the article seemed to be endorsing the essential features of the current electoral system. It is significant, however, that at the very time when he was writing it Mackintosh could say with regard to reform in a letter to Lord Holland: 'Something substantial and serious must be proposed. Without such a plan I doubt whether the country can be kept quiet and whether you can become Ministers. I am sure you cannot without a measure of that sort continue Ministers.' (British Library, Add. MSS 51653, f. 103, Sir James Mackintosh to Lord Holland, 22 December [1818].) Two years later, in another article for the *Edinburgh Review* (November 1820), he indicated the sort of plan he favoured. He suggested that the disparity which had grown up between the system of representation and the distribution of wealth and population might be largely remedied if twenty members were added to the House of Commons, elected by the largest and richest towns which had not hitherto returned MPs; and he also proposed that measures should be taken to facilitate the disfranchisement of boroughs convicted of corruption, an operation which had proved very difficult to accomplish through existing procedures. Around 1820, the view that the party should adopt a more popular stance and a more affirmative attitude to reform was gaining ground among Whig politicians. They did improve their standing with the public by playing a conspicuous part in the movement of protest against the Peterloo massacre and by supporting the cause of Queen Caroline against her husband. At the same period J. G. Lambton (later Earl of Durham) was writing to his father-in-law Grey: 'It is actual insanity to think that we have any chance of turning the Ministers out while the House of Commons is constituted as it is' (Smith, 1975, p. 63); and Lord John Russell was taking the initiative on the reform question in parliament. In December 1819 he moved a resolution – which was accepted by the government – for the disfranchisement of Grampound, a corrupt Cornish borough; in 1821 he put forward proposals similar to Mackintosh's, which were rejected by the narrow margin of 155 votes to 124; and in the following year (on 25 April) he presented a bolder scheme whereby a hundred new members, sixty representing counties and forty representing large towns, would be added to the House, while each of the hundred smallest boroughs would lose one of its two members.

In his speech on this occasion, Russell emphasized the changes which had occurred in the previous forty years: the growth in the wealth of the country and in the importance of the middle classes, and the great diffusion of knowledge evinced by the increased number and circulation of newspapers and periodicals and by the spread of monitorial schools and circulating libraries. Meanwhile, he said, the extent to which public opinion could express itself through the electoral system had if anything contracted as a result of the encroachments of private and ministerial patronage. He alluded to a theory of the constitution which had become fashionable in recent decades: the theory that the balance between king, Lords and Commons was no longer a relationship between separate estates of the realm but was located within the House of Commons, where a smoothly operating system of mutual checks had been established between representatives of the Crown, the peerage and the people. Although some Whigs had earlier shown a partiality for this theory while defending the constitution against radicals, Russell firmly rejected it, on the ground that it offered no security that the true representatives of the people would not be heavily outnumbered. He went on to argue that on a number of recent issues on which public opinion had been strongly roused against the government, the latter's ability to sustain its majority had depended largely on the votes of members for small boroughs; and he produced statistical evidence to show that the smaller the borough in terms of population the more likely it was to be represented by a government supporter. The great Whig families, of course, had their own share of proprietary boroughs, and Russell suggested that this had 'lessened the energy of their efforts in support of the liberties of the country'. He called upon them to set aside private and selfish interests, and to join in effecting changes which, if safely carried out under their sponsorship, would promote the overriding interest which all property-owners had in the maintenance of social harmony and constitutional stability.

In fact, by the time of this speech most Whig politicians, including magnates such as the Dukes of Devonshire and Grafton, had already declared their support for reform. Fitzwilliam was almost alone in retaining a Burkean hostility towards it, but even he reluctantly allowed his son, Lord Milton, to come out publicly in its favour. Milton was one of several young Whig aristocrats – Lord Althorp was another – who were developing an ardent commitment to parliamentary reform, partly because they regarded the Peterloo affair, the dismissal of Fitzwilliam from his lord lieutenancy for helping to organize a protest against it, the passage of the repressive Six Acts in December 1819 and the trial of Queen Caroline as evidence of a sinister trend towards tyrannical and socially divisive government. (Wasson, 1985.) Another reason for the shift of opinion within the Whig party was the fact that in the early 1820s, owing partly to governmental repression but more fundamentally to an alleviation of distress in the manufacturing districts, the popular agitation for universal suffrage lost most of its impetus. A further reason was that at the same period many country gentlemen were showing a more positive interest in parliamentary reform than they had done previously, at least since the county association movement of the early 1780s. A number of attempts had been made in the early nineteenth century to stimulate such an interest. For example, the Hampden Club had been founded in 1811–12 by a Devonshire country gentleman, Thomas Northmore, with the express purpose of adding 'weight of property' to the reform movement by enlisting a corps of substantial landowners. But the membership had never risen above a hundred or so, and those who did join the club were very untypical members of their class: most country gentlemen, alarmed by Luddism and other popular agitations, were firmly conservative during the second decade of the century. At the beginning of the following decade, however, there was a period of agricultural depression: the production of cereals had increased in relation to the demand for them, and the consequent fall in prices, while benefiting consumers, reduced the incomes of farmers and landowners. The agricultural classes pressed the government for some kind of relief, but obtained very little satisfaction; and in these circumstances some members of the gentry began to call for parliamentary reform as a means of making the political elite more responsive to their demands. This was a type of agitation with which the Whigs could readily associate themselves, and in 1821–3 there was a considerable number of county meetings in which Whigs and country gentlemen combined to demand both concessions for the landed interest and a moderate reform of parliament. After 1823 this campaign faded out as the agricultural depression lifted, and the main political issue that was to preoccupy the political nation for the next five years was the Catholic question, but the early 1820s had seen a significant shift in county opinion as well as an almost unanimous commitment to reform on the part of the Whigs. (A. Mitchell, 1965.)

The Middle Classes and Reform

The 1820s also marked – and this was an additional reason for Whig conversions to reform – an important shift in the attitudes of the urban middle classes. The background to this needs to be traced back some way.

In the parliamentary reform movements of the 1780s and 1790s, the bulk of the commercial and industrial middle classes had been little involved; but in the late eighteenth and early nineteenth centuries, one particular circle of people was developing a sense of shared interests and values which foreshadowed a kind of middle-class consciousness. This circle was defined partly by religious affiliation. Almost all the substantial towns of England contained groups of business and professional men who subscribed to 'rational Dissent', especially Unitarianism; and these groups were closely bound together by educational background (at Dissenting academies), by intermarriage and by common intellectual concerns which were fostered by provincial literary and philosophical societies and London-based Unitarian periodicals. In a number of towns, such as Liverpool and Leeds, men of this type were largely excluded from local government, which was in the hands of self-perpetuating Anglican elites; and on the national stage very few Dissenters achieved prominence as politicians. The inquiring and anti-authoritarian cast of mind that was characteristic of the rational Dissenters, together with resentment at the restriction of their civil rights and opportunities, made them natural opponents of oligarchy and privilege; and during the French wars these attitudes were reinforced by economic considerations. Many merchants and manufacturers in the north and midlands felt that their interests were being adversely affected by the uncertainties of war and were being subordinated to the interests of people such as City financiers and West India merchants who had close links with the political establishment. Provincial discontent expressed itself through petitioning movements for peace in 1807–8 and 1812–13, and through the campaign against the Orders in Council in 1812, when the government's measures of economic warfare against Napoleon were disrupting trade with North America. Liberal Dissenters who were prominent in business – William Roscoe in Liverpool, Josiah Wedgwood in the Potteries, Ebenezer Rhodes in Sheffield – played a leading part in these campaigns, though in the one which was successful (against the Orders in Council) they had the valuable co-operation of men such as Thomas Attwood and Richard Spooner of Birmingham, who were Anglican bankers. In these wartime movements the potentially divisive issue of parliamentary reform was generally kept in the background, but several of the liberal Dissenters did declare their support for it. Roscoe, for example, advocated household suffrage in a pamphlet published in 1811, and Edward Baines, editor of the *Leeds Mercury*, maintained that 'a full, free and impartial Representation of the People in parliament, would, by preventing the frequency, and diminishing the duration of wars, increase

11

the commerce and reduce the burthens of the country'. (Read, 1961, p. 109; Cookson, 1982.)

The passage of the Corn Law in 1815, in spite of a massive urban petitioning movement against it, increased the feeling among middle-class liberals that parliament was inattentive to their interests and opinions. In the post-war years, the growth of support for reform among the middle classes was hindered by the factors which were alarming the Whigs at the same period. Although Baines and some others spoke out against extremism and in favour of moderate reform, such voices tended to be swamped during the mass agitations of 1816–17 and 1819. After Peterloo, however, middle-class reformers came into greater prominence. A group of them in Manchester, led by John Edward Taylor, the Unitarian cotton merchant who was to become first editor of the *Manchester Guardian* in 1821, orchestrated local indignation against the conduct of the authorities and had their views expressed in parliament by the Whig reformer H. G. Bennet. Earlier, despite the fact that the Whigs were more sympathetic than the ministerialists to the Dissenters' claims for complete religious toleration, urban liberals had often viewed the parliamentary Whigs rather distrustfully, as a power-seeking aristocratic faction which paid only lip service to reform. But there had been some co-operation with the progressive section of the Whig party known as the 'Mountain', especially with Henry Brougham over the Orders in Council; and such co-operation grew after 1819 as the Whigs showed an increasing commitment to a reform which would involve (among other things) greater representation for urban interests. In 1820 Russell proposed that the seats made available by the disfranchisement of Grampound should be transferred to Leeds; and he said in another speech in the same year (14 March) that county members, however well disposed, were not likely to be able to represent the interests of large towns effectively, because they did not have 'the knowledge requisite for stating the grievances and the wants of manufacturers'. As a result of an amendment in the House of Lords the Grampound seats were in fact transferred to the county of Yorkshire, but in 1826 the Whig gentry agreed that John Marshall of Leeds, a wealthy Unitarian flax-spinner, should stand alongside Lord Milton as a Whig candidate for the county. After the 1826 general election there were Whig-sponsored proposals that the seats of two other corrupt boroughs, Penryn and East Retford, should be transferred to Manchester and Birmingham respectively. Again, these transfers were not effected, but while the proposals were before parliament strong support for them was manifested in the towns concerned, and it became apparent that in these places the belief that great manufacturing and commercial centres needed direct representation was no longer confined to coteries of liberal Dissenters but had come to be held by many businessmen who had previously been apolitical or 'Tory'. An intensification of such feelings was only to be expected when, as happened towards the end of the decade, the economic situation deteriorated. The Birmingham *Argus*, a traditionally loyalist newspaper, said in March 1829: 'The very serious losses to which the trade of Birmingham has been exposed ... might have been greatly diminished, if not entirely prevented, had we been so fortunate as to have possessed two FAITHFUL REPRESENTATIVES IN PARLIAMENT during the last thirty or forty years.' (Briggs, 1948, pp. 193–4.)

No doubt the reasons why support for reform was spreading in middle-class circles were largely pragmatic. But there were also developments in ideology which, by the 1820s, were helping to give the middle classes a sense of collective identity and confidence and a willingness to question the aristocracy's virtual monopoly of political power. Ricardo's brand of economic theory, for instance, helped to promote such attitudes. Whereas in the analyses of Adam Smith and Malthus the economic interests of landowners were generally considered to be in harmony with those of the rest of the community, Ricardo believed that there was a basic conflict of interest between landowners and other classes. He maintained that in a country which produced its own food and had a growing population, there must be a tendency for rents to rise and for profits to fall. As more and more land, of a less and less fertile nature, was brought into cultivation to feed the increasing population, the rents payable to the owners of the more fertile land would steadily rise. At the same time, the application of labour and capital to land would be subject to diminishing returns, the price of food would rise with rising average costs of production, money wages would have to be raised to ensure the continued subsistence of the labourer, and the profits of farmers and capitalists would decline. If these trends were allowed to continue, the accumulation of capital would slow down and the economy would move towards stagnation. According to this analysis, what threatened most directly to arrest the growth of Britain's prosperity was agricultural protection; if this could be abandoned or modified, and manufactured exports could be exchanged for imports of cheaply-produced foreign grain, the future would be much less bleak. Ricardo also held that the interests of the capitalist, unlike those of the landowner, were closely bound up with those of the community at large, for the capitalist's role as saver and investor was the principal generator of economic progress. The relationship between capital and labour was not basically one of conflicting interests, for both stood to gain from a 'progressive' economy with high profits, a high rate of investment and a high demand for labour.

A doctrine which had close links with Ricardian economics was Benthamite Utilitarianism. James Mill, Bentham's principal English follower, was a close friend of Ricardo and one of the most important expositors of his economic theory, and he was also responsible for converting Ricardo to political radicalism; for this reason Bentham described Ricardo as his 'spiritual grandson'. Benthamite political ideas helped in certain ways to underpin attacks on aristocratic power. But it should be noted that as an ideology for buttressing distinctively middle-class interests and aspirations, Bentham's own political theory was not ideally suitable. The case for political reform which he developed in his later years – after he had become convinced that his schemes for other kinds of reform, especially in the legal sphere, would never be implemented by the existing authorities – rested on a combination of three principles. According to the first of these, which he called the 'principle of self-preference', it was a fact of human nature that individuals tended to pursue their own 'self-regarding' interest in preference to the interests of others. According to the second, each person should generally speaking be regarded as the best judge of his or her own interest. According to the third – the normative 'principle of utility' or 'greatest happiness principle' – the aim which any government ought to pursue was the greatest happiness of the greatest number. It followed from the first principle that the actual end pursued by any government would normally be the happiness of the governors; and it followed from the three principles taken together that the means of securing good government was a contrived 'junction of interests' which would bring 'the particular interest of rulers into accordance with the universal interest'. This junction of interests was to be brought about principally by democratic institutions which would make the wielders of power accountable to the people; and in his *Plan of Parliamentary Reform* published in 1817 he advocated annual elections, secret voting, equal electoral districts and 'virtual universality of suffrage', by which he meant the enfranchisement of adult males who were able to read. As he explained in his *Radical Reform Bill* three years later, he did not consider that a reading test involved 'exclusion', since anyone who really wanted to obtain the qualification could do so within a few months. But he felt that a property qualification, such as householdership or payment of direct taxes, did involve exclusion, and was inadmissible because it would prevent a substantial section of the population from obtaining the security for its interests which a due share of representation would provide. He also believed that on the same principle women were entitled to the vote as well as men, though he considered that to put forward such a proposal in the current state of public opinion would retard the cause of radical reform by exposing it to ridicule.

While it will be apparent that Bentham's ideas on reform were too radical to commend themselves easily to the bulk of middle-class opinion, one should add that they were made somewhat more acceptable to such an audience by James Mill, in the *Essay on Government* which he wrote for the *Encyclopaedia Britannica* in 1820 and subsequently published as a pamphlet. Mill, for one thing, did not insist that universal suffrage was necessary in order to produce the required identity of interest between the community and its elected representatives. He suggested that not only women and children but also men under the age of forty, and even those without a certain modicum of property, *might* be excluded from the electorate without seriously weakening the securities for good government. Moreover, in the closing pages of his essay he argued that even if the franchise were very widely extended, reform would give the 'middle rank' a dominant position in the political system. He described the middle rank as the wisest part of the community, and maintained that the great majority of the lower classes would be guided in their political opinions by the advice and example of 'that intelligent, that virtuous rank who come the most immediately in contact with them'. Mill's essay, which stated the case for representative government in a very confident and apparently rigorous fashion, had a considerable vogue in the decade after its publication. The *Morning Chronicle*, the daily paper of the liberal middle classes, remarked (27 April 1822) that there was no finer piece of reasoning in the English language, and the essay was said to have made a great impact on undergraduates at Cambridge in the 1820s. None the less it is possible that the most important contribution of the Utilitarian philosophers to the growth of reformist sentiment within the middle classes lay not so much in any positive arguments they put forward in favour of parliamentary reform, as in their criticisms of oligarchical government.

Here one returns to the pioneering work of Bentham, for no one before him had set out to investigate and expose the evils of oligarchy as systematically as he did in the last twenty years or so of his life. He had originally been preoccupied with abuses in the law, and with the devices used by judges and lawyers in order to mystify the public and enhance their own emoluments; but he had come to see that the political system and the established Church were also riddled with abuses, and that a general partnership existed in which all those who were 'unduly favoured by the laws and habits of government' combined to defend their various 'sinister interests' against inquiry and reform. The monarch was seen as the leading figure in this partnership, as was indicated by the title 'Corruptor-General and Co.' which Bentham gave to it. But the class which profited most extensively from the system, both through its access to official patronage and through its control of legislation, was the landowning aristocracy, which Bentham regarded as an essentially parasitic class. He wrote in a tract of 1821 (*Observations on the Restrictive and Prohibitory Commercial System*):

In England, all other particular interests are overborne and crushed by one great particular interest, named in the aggregate the agricultural interest. By a system of prohibition foreign grain is excluded with the avowed intent of making home-produced grain dearer than it would be otherwise, – dearer to the whole population in the character of consumers and customers; and for the avowed purpose of securing to a particular class of persons a pecuniary advantage, at the expense of the whole population of the country. But the class meant to be favoured, and actually favoured, by this undue advantage, are not any class of persons employed in any beneficial operation; but a class of persons who, without any labour of their own, derive from the labours of others a share of the means of enjoyment much greater than is possessed by any who employ their labour in the purchase of it. They are land proprietors, deriving their means of enjoyment or of luxury from the

16

rent of land cultivated by the industrious: they are in a word, not labourers, but idlers; not the many but the few.

With regard to the means whereby the 'ruling few' maintained their dominance over the 'subject many', Bentham put particular emphasis on the roles of 'corruption' and 'delusion'. By corruption he meant the creation of attitudes of attachment and obsequiousness through the distribution of patronage and other favours. By delusion he meant the process whereby the ruling few, through their influence over opinion-forming agencies such as the Church, educational institutions, and the press, induced the subject many to accept and even respect the established ·mode of government and distribution of power. The work of his which reached the largest English-speaking audience in the early nineteenth century – partly at second hand through Sydney Smith's witty summary of it in the *Edinburgh Review* – was the *Book of Fallacies* (1824), in which he exposed the speciousness of many types of argument used by upholders of the system and opponents of reform.

Bentham's efforts to combat 'delusion' and to open people's eyes to the partiality and privilege ingrained in the country's institutions were seconded by other Utilitarian publications of the 1820s, such as the *Westminster Review*, a quarterly started (with financial aid from Bentham himself) in 1824, and the *Parliamentary History and Review*, a serial launched in 1825, which printed reports of the parliamentary debates along with a commentary pointing out the fallacious arguments used in them. An article on 'Reform of Parliament' in the first volume of the latter review described the landowners, who were enabled by the system of open voting to exercise a dominant influence over elections, as 'a class of men whose interests are more irreconcilably opposed to those of the rest of the community than the interests of any other class whatever'; and James Mill, in the first issue of the *Westminster*, argued that the Church, the legal profession, and the universities (which were a mere subdivision of the Church) were 'props' of the oligarchy of some 200 families which controlled a majority of seats in the House of Commons. (Hamburger, 1965, pp. 41–2; Thomas, 1969, pp. 265–6.) Some educated people were repelled by the dogmatic and abrasive tone adopted by Utilitarian critics of the English political system; but there is no doubt that Benthamite ideas had a strong appeal for many members of the rising middle classes, who found the

17

principle of utility a valuable weapon for use against institutions and procedures which they regarded as archaic, irrational and exclusive. In particular, Bentham's thought attracted many Unitarian radicals, although his own hostility to religion went far beyond their rejection of orthodox Trinitarian doctrine. Archibald Prentice wrote in his newspaper, the *Manchester Gazette*, in December 1825: 'Believing that the object of legislation and government ought to be to produce THE GREATEST HAPPINESS OF THE GREATEST NUMBER, we shall, in all our political discussions, keep that object before us, as a land mark towards which to steer amidst the storm of contending parties.' (Read, 1958, p. 62.) T. A. Ward, cutlery manufacturer and editor of the *Sheffield Independent* in the 1820s, was another avowed Benthamite; and John Marshall of Leeds was so impressed by the *Book of Fallacies* that he provided the funds to set up the *Parliamentary History and Review*. The question of what part Benthamite ideas played subsequently in the Reform Bill crisis will be discussed in chapter 3, but first we shall examine the ideas associated with *popular* radicalism in the twenty years before 1830, looking incidentally at the extent to which Utilitarian theories were absorbed at that level.

2 Popular Radicalism
c.1810–29

The term 'popular radicalism' is used here to cover the more or less democratic brands of radicalism which had a wide appeal for people of little or no property. Some of its outstanding spokesmen came from 'higher' social strata: Sir Francis Burdett was a wealthy landowner and baronet, Major John Cartwright came from a family of country gentlemen, Henry Hunt was a gentleman-farmer. Cartwright himself, and even more incongruously the Duke of Richmond, had supplied the basic programme of reform which the London Corresponding Society and other artisan societies had adopted in the 1790s, and similarly in the second decade of the nineteenth century some of the ideas and arguments of the popular reform movement were provided by 'outsiders'. None the less, in a basic sense the movement's driving force – especially after the end of the French wars – derived from perceptions and aspirations that were emerging within the working classes.

The story of radicalism in the 1790s and, in so far as it then survived, in the 1800s has been admirably summarized by H. T. Dickinson in an earlier study in the present series (1985). The democratic agitation of the period of the French Revolution reached its first peak in 1792, the year which saw the publication of the second part of Thomas Paine's *Rights of Man*, the revolution of 10 August in Paris, and the first substantial working-class organizations devoted to the cause of parliamentary reform in Britain. There was a second peak during the subsistence crisis of 1795, but at no stage in these years did the movement attract *mass* support; except in one or two places such as Sheffield and Norwich the radicals were conscious of facing either apathy or hostility from the bulk of the population. After 1795, public agitation for reform encountered almost insuperable obstacles: in particular, the repressive legislation passed by Pitt's government, and the waves of loyalist sentiment which were aroused, especially in 1796–8 and 1803–5, by the threat of a French invasion. It is true that in the years around the turn of the century, there was a hard core of ultra-radicals in England, many of them expatriate Irishmen, who formed underground organizations and hoped to achieve a revolution in England and Ireland through a combination of popular risings and a French landing. Also, there may have been a considerable amount of *passive* disaffection among the politically inarticulate classes, which suffered an unusual degree of hardship at this time.

However, on the surface there was more or less general support for the war effort, and political dissent was extremely muted. It was only after the battle of Trafalgar, which reduced the pressure for national unity by removing the danger of invasion, that there was a gradual revival of public interest in reform. This was fuelled by resentment at the high level of wartime taxation and by a feeling that the war was being inefficiently conducted. In addition, distrust of the political elite was heightened by the fact that when the Foxite Whigs were in office in 1806–7 they did nothing to honour their earlier pledges to effect a 'change of system'; the *Edinburgh Review* had to admit in July 1807 that there was 'a very general spirit of discontent, distrust and contempt for public characters, among the more intelligent and resolute portion of the inferior ranks of society'.

Burdettite Radicalism and Luddism

Around 1810, the most prominent champions of parliamentary reform were Burdett and Cartwright, together with the journalist William Cobbett. They were anxious not to provoke a new outbreak of the anti-Jacobin alarmism which had been aroused against the radicals of the 1790s, and they were not calling for universal suffrage as the London Corresponding Society had done. Cartwright told Christopher Wyvill in 1808 that although he was still privately attached to this principle he was prepared to work for a more limited reform; and the programme which he shortly afterwards espoused was the one outlined by Burdett in the House of Commons in June 1809, comprising annual parliaments, equal electoral districts, and the enfranchisement of all men subject to direct taxation. Burdett had been returned to parliament for Westminster in 1807 through the efforts of a committee of local tradesmen, including several former members of the London Corresponding Society, who put him forward as an independent candidate in opposition to the two established parties. Westminster, a 'scot and lot' borough, had a largely petit bourgeois electorate of rate-paying householders, which was to remain loyal to Burdett for thirty years. For some time, he also had a large following of working men, inside and outside the metropolis, which he earned through speaking out boldly and almost alone in the House of Commons against the damaging effects of the war and the 'boroughmongering system' on the people at large. He argued that it was owing to the lack of a real representation of the people in parliament that excessive taxes were laid upon them to pay for unnecessary wars and for the luxurious maintenance of a host of placemen and pensioners. By attributing the burden of taxation not only to the war but also to 'corruption', he was able to link his demand for parliamentary reform to a central theme of the time-honoured 'country' or 'patriot' ideology professed by eighteenth-century opposition groups. Alongside concern about corruption, another feature of that ideology had been concern about standing armies and the repressive use that could be made of them; and this was another theme which appeared in Burdett's speeches. During the Luddite disturbances of 1812, after troops and militiamen had been used against the rioters, Burdett said (1 May) that the government was employing the army for 'the subjugation of the people' in defiance of 'the constitutional opinions of our ancestors'. (Dinwiddy, 1980.)

In many ways, it is a far cry from Burdett's old-fashioned and rather patrician style of 'patriotism' to machine-breaking in south Lancashire or the Calder valley. Although Burdett urged that the Luddites should be treated leniently, he did not condone their resort to violence. Nor did Major Cartwright: indeed in a letter published in the *Nottingham Review* in January 1812 he said that nothing was more likely to strengthen the hands of the borough faction. Luddism, the series of machine-breaking incidents that occurred in the north and midlands in 1811–12, was an indigenous working-class agitation that developed quite independently of the leaders of popular radicalism. It had a variety of causes. In all three of the industries involved – the east midlands hosiery trade, the west Yorkshire woollen trade and the Lancashire cotton trade – artisans were facing serious threats to their status and living standards, owing partly to an overstocking of the labour market and partly to the introduction of machines or manufacturing techniques which devalued their skills; and in all three industries they had tried unsuccessfully to obtain protection for their interests by appealing to the law

21

or to parliament. In the woollen trade, for example, the cloth-makers had conducted a long campaign to secure the enforcement of certain Tudor statutes, including one which prohibited the use of 'gig mills' for finishing cloth, but the masters had mounted a counter-campaign and the outcome had been the repeal in 1809 of the statutes which the workers had wished to see enforced. In the cotton industry, the handloom weavers had applied to parliament in 1807–8 for minimum-wage legislation covering their trade, but although a bill for this purpose had been introduced in the Commons it had soon been dropped in the face of strong opposition; and a further application for some means of relief in 1811 had met with a thoroughly negative response from a select committee.

It was in the wake of frustrations such as these – and in the particularly severe economic conditions of 1811–12 – that the framework-knitters, clothdressers and handloom weavers turned to machine-breaking as a means of extorting concessions from their employers. At the same period, there were people in these industrial areas, especially in the northern counties, who favoured political agitation. In the years around the turn of the century a certain amount of underground political activity had taken place in Lancashire and Yorkshire, where oath-bound societies had been formed on the model of the republican Society of United Irishmen. In 1812, some people were trying to revive this kind of conspiracy and graft it on to Luddism. They were probably helped by the fact that two major Luddite attacks on factories in April – one at Rawfolds in the West Riding and one at Middleton to the north of Manchester – were beaten off, and by the fact that on both occasions the assailants were faced not only by the factory-owners and their men but also by militiamen brought in to guard the mills. These incidents may have helped to give an insurrectionary turn to the agitation, by bringing it home to the Luddites that they were in confrontation with the state as well as the masters. There is evidence from both Lancashire and Yorkshire that in the summer of 1812 the administration of secret oaths became associated with talk of a 'general rising' of the people and with the seizure of fire-arms from private houses. However, the revolutionary impulse does not appear to have been very formidable or sustained. By the late summer, after the authorities had made several arrests and the economic situation had begun to improve, oath-taking as well as machine-breaking seems to have petered out in the northern counties.

There were also some people during the period of Luddism,

22

at least in the north west, who were recommending pressure for parliamentary reform. In 1811–12 a committee of representatives of trades in the Manchester area – encouraged by John Knight, a small manufacturer who was to have a long career in radical politics – was trying to arrange a petition to the Commons for peace and reform. This attempt was scotched in June 1812 when the deputy constable of Manchester raided a meeting and arrested those present on a charge (which was subsequently refuted in court) of administering unlawful oaths. The proceedings of the committee showed, however, that the demand for reform was being directly linked to the grievances of industrial workers and to parliament's failure to redress them. A printed address issued in October 1811, and composed by Knight, referred to the *laissez-faire* conclusions of the Commons committee on the weavers' petitions earlier in the year and went on to say:

> They, the Members of that House, can make arrangements which advance the price of provisions – increase your taxes – introduce such a state of things as diminishes your business and employment, and reduces your wages, and when you state to them that you cannot exist under these accumulated and accumulating evils, they then coolly tell you they *cannot* relieve you. Had you possessed 70,000 votes for the election of Members to sit in that House, would your application have been treated with such indifference, not to say inattention? We believe not. (Hammond and Hammond, 1919, pp. 84–5.)

Subsequently, further evidence of the unresponsiveness of parliament to the demands of working men for some form of protection was to be provided by the repeal of the apprenticeship clauses of the Elizabethan Statute of Artificers. In 1813 an artisans' organization asked parliament to ensure that these clauses, which confined the workforce of the traditional trades to men who had served (or were serving) seven-year apprenticeships, were more effectively enforced to prevent the trades concerned from being flooded with relatively unskilled labour. But parliament proceeded in the following session to *repeal* the relevant clauses, despite petitions signed by some 300,000 people urging their retention.

Meanwhile, Cartwright had been waging a single-handed campaign to arouse interest in reform in the manufacturing districts.

Disappointed by his earlier attempts to enlist co-operation from members of the propertied classes, he had resolved in 1812 to see whether the discontents which lay behind Luddism could be redirected into 'a legal channel favourable to parliamentary reform'. Making two extensive tours through the provinces within six months, he had considerable success in securing support for reform petitions on Burdett's plan, even though this plan (confining the franchise to those who paid direct taxes) did not have much of immediate value to offer the working classes. By May 1813, some 200,000 signatures had been collected for such petitions, including 30,000 from Manchester and 17,000 from Halifax.

The Revival of Universal Suffrage

After the end of the war there was a dramatic extension of working-class interest in political reform. The economic depression of 1816–17, even more widespread than that of 1811–12, was particularly resented because people had hoped for better things when peace eventually came. John Knight said in a letter to Lord Sidmouth, the Home Secretary, in 1817 that what had 'raised dissatisfaction to its zenith, was, that when the War was o'er and People expected, as usual, plenty to have returned with Peace, their sufferings became greater than ever'. He added that 'at that juncture, the Populace would have fallen upon their Employers or the Dealers in Provisions, or both; but for the views exhibited by the advocates of Parliamentary Reform'. (Public Record Office, HO 42/168, John Knight to Viscount Sidmouth, 17 July 1817.) From November 1816, when Cobbett began republishing the leading article of his *Weekly Political Register* as a separate twopenny pamphlet, the message that parliamentary reform was the key to an improvement in the condition of the people was being transmitted directly to a large working-class audience. Samuel Bamford wrote later in his *Passages in the Life of a Radical* that in the winter of 1816–17 Cobbett's writings were being read in nearly every cottage in south Lancashire and the east midlands. 'Their influence was speedily visible; he directed his readers to the true cause of their sufferings – misgovernment; and to its proper corrective – parliamentary reform. Riots soon became scarce, and from that time they have never obtained their ancient vogue with the labourers of this country.'

Why were so many working men persuaded that parliamentary

reform was worth seeking? No doubt one reason for this development – though it was also in part a consequence of it – was the readoption by prominent reformers of a genuinely democratic programme. The man who led the way in this respect was Henry Hunt, who had been making a reputation for himself as a radical orator in the preceding years. He was the main speaker at a large popular meeting which took place in Spa Fields, London, on 2 December 1816, and the petition which was framed by him and approved by the meeting called for annual parliaments and universal suffrage, 'seeing that all men pay taxes, and that all men have lives and liberties to protect'. Meanwhile at the instigation of the Hampden Club, which had shrunk to a handful of active members but which Cartwright had been using as an institutional base for his efforts to arouse radical activity, a large number of local Hampden Clubs were springing up in the provinces, especially in Lancashire and the east midlands; and as a preliminary to the presentation of a great quantity of reform petitions to parliament at the beginning of the 1817 session, a meeting of deputies from petitioning bodies in the country was held in London on 22 January. A number of the deputies had been instructed by the working-class clubs and communities which they represented to press for universal rather than a more limited suffrage, and when it was proposed in the name of the original Hampden Club that a programme of annual parliaments and *household* suffrage should be pursued, the meeting carried by a large majority an amendment in favour of universal suffrage, moved by Hunt and supported by Samuel Bamford of Middleton. Cartwright and Cobbett had initially supported the household suffrage proposal, out of deference to Burdett who had indicated that this was as far as he was prepared to go; but they accepted and probably welcomed the decision of the meeting, and thereafter were strong advocates of the more radical measure.

It is not difficult to understand why a predominantly working-class movement for reform should have chosen universal suffrage as its principal goal in preference to a more restricted franchise. It is harder to answer the more fundamental question, which the change of programme is not in itself enough to explain, of why working men in the post-war years should have become so receptive to the message of Cobbett and others that the 'proper corrective' for their sufferings was *political* reform. Part of the answer must lie in the failure or ineffectiveness of other strategies. Direct action had been tried with very little positive result. Luddism, suppressed in 1812, was briefly revived in Nottinghamshire and Leicestershire in 1816, but was again suppressed with the help of several executions. It had never had much success, except occasionally in the very short term, as a means of preventing cost-reducing changes in methods of production. The year 1816 also saw an outbreak of fierce agrarian rioting, prompted by high food prices and unemployment, in East Anglia; and this too was crushed with some severity. In most parts of the country, especially the industrialized ones, food riots were ceasing to be common. In the eighteenth century they had been the most usual form of collective protest in times of dearth; and in relatively small-scale communities where magistrates were often more inclined to mediate between the crowd and the dealers in provisions than to resort to military and judicial repression, this type of pressure had offered some prospect of relief. But the alarms created by the French Revolution and Painite radicalism had hardened the attitudes of the propertied classes towards popular violence; and in urban or semi-urban environments, where communications between the authorities and the populace were often tenuous, the tacit conventions and reciprocal restraints which had facilitated local 'bargaining by riot' over food prices no longer functioned in the same way. (Bohstedt, 1983, chapter 9.)

By contrast, peaceful methods of collective bargaining, focused on wages rather than prices, were being more widely used in the early nineteenth century. The fact that, between the passage of the Combination Acts in 1799–1800 and their repeal in 1824, trade unions were illegal under statute as well as common law did not prevent the continuation of their long-term growth. Indeed in a number of industries, such as the London handicraft trades, conditions of high demand and full employment produced a marked strengthening of trade unionism during the Napoleonic wars; and some artisan groups in the provinces, such as the hatters of north-east Cheshire, had combinations strong enough to insist on the retention of a strict apprenticeship system. Nevertheless there were a number of factors, some of them particularly evident in the post-war years, which limited the scope and effectiveness of trade union action as a means of protecting living standards. The most important underlying factor was the almost permanent surplus of labour which existed in many areas as a result of the high rate of population growth. This was especially serious for outworkers in the textile industries. Being geographically scattered rather than concentrated in factories, and having skills which were not very hard to acquire, they had difficulty in organizing effectively and controlling entry to their trades; and it was only in exceptional boom years that they could attempt strike action in the hope of retrieving some of the ground lost at other times through wage reductions. Even in London an abundant supply of labour and a widening of the market were helping to produce a 'dishonourable' or non-unionized sector in the traditional handicraft trades such as tailoring and cabinet-making: a sector in which 'foul' masters employed semi-skilled workers at wages below the customary level. These workers were especially vulnerable in trade depressions such as that of 1816–17; and the existence of this sector threatened the ability of the trade societies in the 'honourable' sector to maintain the status and wage-levels of the skilled artisans. (Prothero, 1979, chapter 2.)

There can be no doubt that many workers turned to parliamentary reform because of their weakness in the industrial sphere, and because they believed that state power was contributing to that weakness when it could be used to protect them. This was particularly evident in the case of the handloom weavers in the north west. In the early 1790s, they had still been enjoying a prosperity which resulted from the fact that the spinning side of the cotton industry was mechanized before the weaving side and the increase in the output of spun yarn expanded the demand for weavers' labour. But since then too many people had entered the trade, and incipient competition from power-looms had helped to cause a drastic fall in piece-rates. Handloom weavers were much involved in the Lancashire Hampden Clubs of 1816–17. In the temporarily improved conditions of 1818, some concessions were extracted from the employers by a weavers' strike, despite the arrest and subsequent imprisonment of three of its leaders. But these gains were nullified in the depression of the following year; and in June 1819 the weavers' committee at Stockport declared in an address to the local magistrates that they had decided to back the campaign for parliamentary reform because all other ways of seeking an improvement of their condition had failed. 'The fate of their ... petitions and memorials to Parliament is so well known as not to require description. By those [from] whom the weavers sought protection they have been rewarded with punishment.' (Read, 1958, p. 23; Glen, 1984, chapters 9–10.)

The grievances of industrial workers, and the kind of remedial measures which they wished to see adopted by the legislature, varied considerably from trade to trade. The handloom weavers, in addition to minimum-wage regulations of the kind established for the London silkweavers in the 1770s, wanted a prohibition of the export of cotton twist. The framework-knitters, led by Gravener Henson, wanted statutory endorsement for a variety of customary practices which maintained standards of production and protected workers against exploitation in the hosiery trade. At the same time there were some notable advocates of parliamentary reform who wanted the state to interfere *less* in economic and industrial matters, rather than more. The Westminster radical Francis Place (a former journeyman and member of the London Corresponding Society who had become a master-tailor) was among those who campaigned for the *repeal* of the apprenticeship clauses of the Statute of Artificers; and a meeting organized shortly afterwards by the Westminster reformers resolved 'that, among the many calamitous circumstances arising from the want of a real Representation of the People ... is to be reckoned the evil of excessive Legislation; or, in other words, the interference of Parliament in matters which cannot advantageously be regulated by law, and in which, therefore, the exertions of individuals ought to be left free and unrestrained.' (*Statesman*, 8 March 1815.) In the face of such diversity it made quite good sense for the reformers to follow the advice given by Cobbett in his *Political Register* on 26 October 1816; he said that since many evils existed, and they could all – in so far as they were curable – be cured by a parliamentary reform, attention should be concentrated on this 'great and single object' rather than on its hoped-for consequences.

There was one evil, however, which *all* supporters of radical reform hoped that it would relieve: the burden of taxation. By Cobbett, Hunt, Burdett, and many others, this was seen as the basic cause of popular distress. Indeed, the increase in the amount of revenue raised annually through taxes, from £16 or £17 million before the war to between £50 and £60 million in the years after 1815, was striking. The radicals argued that taxation – mostly in the form of indirect taxes on ordinary articles of consumption – not only cut deeply into working-class incomes but also contributed to economic depression and unemployment: it reduced the effective demand for manufactured goods, and thereby reduced the demand for labour. Also, of course, for them taxation was the link between popular hardship and politics. Unlike other causes of distress – such as harvest-failure, or a disappointing level of foreign demand for British manufactures, or the population growth which the followers of

Malthus were emphasizing – the fiscal burden could be squarely attributed to the government and legislature. The idea that the essence of the English political system was a great fleecing operation whereby money was transferred from the pockets of the people into the pockets of the office-holding class had been current in the 1790s; but in the post-war years it was even more prevalent. A series of publications such as *The Extraordinary Red Book* and *The Black Book: or Corruption Unmasked* provided a wealth of detail about the sums received by placemen and pensioners and about the family relationships which connected many of these people together. The attack on 'Old Corruption' was emotive and easily grasped; it suited the oratorical style of Henry Hunt, who thundered against those who 'fattened on the plunder of the people'; and it suited the journalism of Cobbett, who liked to personalize political issues and sniped continuously at conspicuous official pluralists. Cobbett, moreover, helped to give a further dimension to the critique of taxation by drawing attention to the fiscal burden imposed by the greatly expanded National Debt. He put the 'fundholders' (who received interest on holdings of government stock) into the category of parasitic 'taxeaters' along with placemen and pensioners; and at a time when the servicing of the debt was absorbing some 80 per cent of the national revenue this point carried considerable force.

There were some people who wished to extend the attack on parasites by including in this category not only placemen and fundholders but also those who lived off rents derived from land. Such a view had been propagated by Thomas Spence, the diminutive and unworldly publicist from Newcastle who from the 1770s onwards had persistently urged that land should be transferred from private ownership to communal control. An article in his short-lived paper *The Giant-Killer* (13 August 1814) pointed out that, according to a recent calculation, the total rent of land and houses amounted to just over £40 million, while the income of stockholders amounted to £19 million; given a total population of 10.5 million, this meant a 'tax or burden' of £6 per year on every man, woman and child, 'merely to support these drones in luxury and pomp'. After his death in 1814, Spence's ideas about the abolition of private property in land retained a certain following, and had some influence on the group of ultra-radicals which centred around James Watson and Arthur Thistlewood. Opponents of radicalism liked to claim (as in the reports of parliamentary committees of secrecy in 1817) that Spencean ideas were rife in the popular reform movement;

and it is true that the belief that the land ought to be 'restored' to the people was deeply rooted in the popular mind. However, leaders of the reform movement such as Hunt were careful to dissociate themselves from plans for the abolition or redistribution of property, and in general in post-war radical propaganda attacks on members of the aristocracy as owners of land and recipients of rent were much less common than attacks on them as the principal controllers and beneficiaries of a corrupt political system.

Legitimation and Militancy

Something has now been said about the material grievances and expectations which lay behind popular radicalism in the second decade of the century. What of the more abstract ideas that were sources of inspiration or legitimation in this movement? Some notable radicals were influenced by the doctrine of natural rights which had been widely current in late eighteenth-century Europe. The veteran Major Cartwright, for example, was apt to speak of political liberty as 'a sacred right of nature', and in spite of his temporary retreat to a more moderate position in 1808 he was again using this concept after the war to justify manhood suffrage. Also, the young Richard Carlile, embarking on his career as a political journalist in partnership with William Sherwin in 1817–18, became a devotee of Thomas Paine's ideas, and *Sherwin's Weekly Political Register* repeatedly asserted that all power which did not emanate from the people was contrary to the rights of man. However, many reformers of the post-war period were chary of emphasizing ideas which were associated in people's minds with the French Revolution, and the pure doctrine of natural rights was less commonly invoked than other concepts of rights which seemed less metaphysical and less foreign. One such concept was that of the rights of labour. Radical publicists had not as yet adopted anything that deserved the name of a labour theory of value; but they certainly believed in a general way that labour was the basic source of wealth, and that in view of this the labouring classes had at least as good a claim as other sections of the community to enjoy political rights. In his widely circulated 'Address to Journeymen and Labourers' (2 November 1816) Cobbett said that 'the real strength and all the resources of a country, ever have sprung and ever must spring, from the *labour* of its people'; and a few weeks later a meeting of radical deputies at Middleton in south Lancashire declared: 'Suffrage commensurate with *direct* Taxation, seems to grant that property only ought to be represented; whereas, labour makes property, and therefore in the name of common sense ought to be represented.' (Belchem, 1978, p. 748.)

The other concept of rights that was much used as a justification for a democratic franchise was the idea of the historic rights of Englishmen: the idea that at some time in the past the English people had enjoyed a free and popular constitution, which they were now simply trying to recover. The notion of reform as a return to an earlier state of purity, or as the restitution of a lost patrimony, had a great appeal in English political culture, as it has had in others. Many people seem to have drawn a stronger sense of legitimation from it than from any other mode of argument. Also, it furnished a response to conservative allegations that the radicals were innovators whose schemes were speculative and impracticable. As Burdett put it in a speech of 2 June 1818: 'If the people claimed rights anciently possessed by their ancestors, and exercised without any ill consequences having been proved to have resulted from their enjoyment, ... no objection could be raised against them as being new, visionary, and wild.' Burdett himself tended to look for precedents in the medieval period: in the same speech of 1818 (one of the few in which he argued unequivocally for universal suffrage) he maintained that an act of Henry IV's reign had recognized the common-law right of all Englishmen to vote at county elections. More commonly, the putatively democratic 'ancient constitution' was located in the Anglo-Saxon period. Major Cartwright was a notable exponent of this idea, and was able to combine it with a belief in the rights of nature because the Anglo-Saxon constitution as he conceived it provided a model which conveniently coincided with his notions of natural right: the witenagemot had been elected annually by universal male suffrage.

A radical thinker who eschewed *both* the idea of natural rights *and* that of historic rights was Jeremy Bentham; and one may ask how far his attempt to propagate alternative arguments based on utility had an influence on the popular reform movement. His abstruse and convoluted style was an obstacle to such influence; Cobbett described his *Plan of Parliamentary Reform* as 'puzzling and tedious beyond mortal endurance'. (Thomas, 1979, p. 29.) But the appearance of an eminent philosopher in the ranks of the radicals was greeted with enthusiasm by some of them, and attempts were made to give publicity to his ideas. T. J. Wooler of the *Black Dwarf* brought out a cheap edition of the *Plan of*

31

Parliamentary Reform in a simplified style 'adapted to the popular reader', and he printed in his newspaper many extracts from other works by Bentham. Even more taken with Bentham's ideas (though one should add that his paper received financial support from Bentham) was John Wade, the former wool-sorter who edited *The Gorgon* in 1818–19. He asserted the superiority of Bentham's political theory over that of Paine, maintaining (in accordance with Bentham's earlier critique of the French 'Declaration of the Rights of Man') that talk of natural rights was vacuous, that meaningful rights were the creation of society and that utility was the basis on which they should be regulated. Few popular radicals, however, wished to *repudiate* the doctrine of the rights of man, and very few of them were attracted by the sort of austere logical reasoning which Bentham used to construct his alternative case. Some would probably have agreed with a point made by Cartwright in an address to the electors of Westminster on 6 April 1819: that those who rested their case for reform on considerations of utility or 'expediency' could not be expected to be as constant in pursuit of universal suffrage as those who were committed to the concept of immutable right. Indeed, there was evidence in Wade's own paper of a willingness to compromise with moderate reformers for the sake of mounting a united campaign of the 'productive classes'. He wrote on 25 July: 'We wish the *Ultra* Reformers, the Universal Suffrage men, to which we belong, to make some advances to the moderate Reformers; and on the other hand we shall expect the latter to come down and meet us with some sacrifices on their part.' He added that he was more concerned about the interests and happiness of the people than he was about their inalienable rights.

As well as criticizing the doctrine of natural rights, Wade attacked those reformers who 'filled the heads of the people with nonsense' about 'the supposed rights and privileges of our ancestors'. On this point, Paine's view had been not dissimilar to Bentham's, and the Painite paper *Sherwin's Political Register* took the same line as *The Gorgon*, denying that speculations about what had existed centuries ago could be of any use 'as an authority for what ought to exist at the present day'. Still, despite these criticisms, and despite several attempts by conservative writers to demonstrate the lack of historical substance in radical interpretations of the 'ancient constitution', this mode of argument proved remarkably tenacious. It is worth noting that even Bentham's follower Francis Place could devote much effort to research on parliamentary history, believing that the antiquity of the reformers' claims was worth establishing because so many people were 'led more by authority than by reason'. (Wallas, 1925, p. 128; Calhoun, 1982, pp. 102–3; Lee, 1982.)

Appeals to history were used by the radicals not only to justify their reform programme but also to justify their ways of campaigning for it. Strictly speaking, such appeals for the latter purpose were not much more valid than they were for the former. Although meetings of counties or corporations, officially convened to petition the king or parliament, were a recognized feature of the constitution, the vast popular meetings which were held by radicals in places such as Spa Fields in London, Newhall Hill outside Birmingham, and St Peter's Fields, Manchester, were an innovation for which precedents could hardly be found, at least before the 1790s. None the less, the freedom of the people to assemble peaceably in order to express their grievances was widely held to be one of the time-honoured rights of Englishmen: Hunt claimed at Spa Fields that it was 'a privilege due to us by the constitution'. (Belchem, 1978, p. 748.) The radicals tried to ensure that their meetings were orderly and could not be branded as breaches of the peace; at the same time they tried to mobilize people in such numbers and to arouse such enthusiasm for the cause that parliament and the ruling classes would be made to feel that resistance was hopeless. When parliament treated large-scale petitioning with indifference, the methods adopted by the radicals for enforcing attention to their demands became more threatening and hovered on the edge of illegality. In the spring of 1817 there was the abortive mass march from the north west to London to present petitions to the Prince Regent in person (the March of the Blanketeers), and in August 1819 there were drilling parties on the moors of south Lancashire in preparation for the great demonstration with drums and banners in St Peter's Fields, Manchester. When the authorities responded to radical agitation by passing repressive legislation, as they did in March 1817 and December 1819, or by taking physical action against the crowd at 'Peterloo', the leaders of the movement were able to heighten their rhetoric and invoke the right of resistance to oppression. There were appeals to the memory of Hampden, Sydney and Russell, and to the idea that the constitution embodied a tacit compact between governors and governed. A radical meeting at Finsbury declared after Peterloo that the social compact was 'broken up' and that a tyrannous government was depriving the people of 'every vestige of the freedom guaranteed to them by their forefathers; and Richard Carlile, who had been on the platform with Hunt in St Peter's Fields, wrote in *Sherwin's Political Register*: 'The People have now no recourse left but to arm themselves immediately, for the recovery of their rights, and the defence of their persons, or patiently to submit to the most unconditional slavery.' (Belchem, 1981, p. 15; Wiener, 1983, p. 42.)

Yet however much radical orators and journalists might claim that the government had overstepped the bounds of constitutional propriety and thereby legitimized resistance, it was extremely difficult to mount such resistance in practice. One of the most basic problems was lack of arms. Radicals often insisted that the *right* of every citizen to bear arms was a part of the ancient constitution, confirmed by the Bill of Rights; but although some pike-making and collecting of guns went on in late 1819 and early 1820, the working population as a whole had very little access to weapons. Burdett protested in a speech of 1816 against any idea of leading the people to 'expose their naked bosoms to balls and bayonets', and he said to J. C. Hobhouse in October 1819 'that it is useless to prompt people to resistance when they have no arms'. (Dinwiddy, 1980, p. 31.) Some ultra-radicals nurtured the dream of an uncontrollable 'general rising', perhaps in support of some sensational coup: Thistlewood and his colleagues in the Cato Street Conspiracy of February 1820 hoped that a collective assassination of the cabinet would excite this kind of popular response. Others believed that concerted preparations were needed before a resort to force could be realistically attempted. In the post-war years there were at least two efforts to arrange a co-ordinated rising in the provinces, one in the north and midlands in the early summer of 1817, and one in the northern counties and the west of Scotland in the spring of 1820. But as soon as radical agitation became conspiratorial, it became vulnerable to penetration by spies: as was particularly evident in May–June 1817, when the authorities were receiving valuable information not only from Oliver, the famous agent employed by the Home Office, but also from others employed by a Sheffield magistrate and the Nottingham town clerk. Furthermore, despite the Hampden Clubs of 1816–17 and a further batch of Union Societies and societies of 'Political Protestants' in 1818–19, the post-war radical movement was never highly organized; and when the agitation went underground, although local networks survived to some extent, it was extremely difficult to establish effective communications among scattered groups of conspirators. The tiny attempts at insurrection which did take place, such as those at Pentrich in Derbyshire in June 1817 and Grange Moor near Huddersfield in April 1820, seem to have been undertaken by people who believed that similar groups would be rising simultaneously elsewhere, when in fact action in other places had been called off.

As well as noting these practical difficulties, one needs to ask how widespread and serious the will to revolution was. Historians have differed widely on this question. J. L. and B. Hammond, 'New Liberals' of the early twentieth century who were pioneers of English social history, regarded the working-class movements of the early nineteenth century as basically constitutionalist and non-violent. They tended to attribute what insurrectionary episodes there were to a handful of hotheads under the influence of *agents provocateurs* (see, for example, 1919, chapter 12), and they maintained that there was no justification for the repressive measures which governments of the time adopted against popular agitation. This interpretation accorded with that put forward in the early nineteenth century by Whig politicians such as H. G. Bennet, and by the respectable radical Francis Place whose voluminous papers have been a very important though somewhat one-sided source for historians. On the other hand, the interpretation of the 'New Left' historian E. P. Thompson in *The Making of the English Working Class* – an extremely forceful book, first published in 1963, which has attracted the interest of countless students to this period as well as having a notable influence on historiography – is very different. Whereas the Hammonds, he says, tended to *start* their research with the assumption that it was highly unlikely that English working men engaged in serious revolutionary conspiracies, he considers that in view of the conditions of the time it would have been more surprising if they had *not* done so. He believes that there *was* a strong revolutionary element in working-class agitation; and he writes of a 'secret revolutionary tradition', a continuous strand of underground politics, running from the 1790s through to the post-war period. He is inclined to glamorize this strand, or at least to show strong sympathy for it: men such as George Mellor, the Luddite who assassinated a Yorkshire manufacturer, and Jeremiah Brandreth, who led the Pentrich rising, are described as being in their own context 'men of heroic stature'. (E. P. Thompson, 1968, pp. 647–8.)

Research carried out by Thompson, or inspired by his

example, has shown that in some places insurrectionary plotting did take place in the years 1817–20, and that it cannot simply be attributed to the instigation of spies. It is clear that besides the Thistlewood group in London there were committed revolutionaries in the provinces such as Thomas Bacon, the silver-haired stockinger from Derbyshire who tried to involve Bamford in the plots preceding the Pentrich rising. It is also clear that in certain communities where artisan groups faced a steady deterioration of income and status – as did the linen-weavers of Barnsley for example, or the framework-knitters of east midlands out-villages – people could be persuaded by local militants to take the very large step from disaffection into rebellion; and although only a few hundred men actually took this step, many more in the same or similar environments may have seriously contemplated it. However, it is possible that those who *were* in such environments – marked by a fair degree of politicization, a strong sense of communal solidarity, and sharply declining prospects – overestimated the number of people in the country at large who shared their anger and aspirations. There is evidence that, although the immediate post-war years did see sharp country-wide fluctuations in economic activity, the long-term fall in prices which began around the end of the Napoleonic wars brought with it an upward trend in average real incomes. Although outworkers (as distinct from skilled factory workers) in the textile industries and the much less politicized class of agricultural workers were faced with increasing adversity, there were other sections of the working population which were making some gains, at least in terms of purchasing power.

A final obstacle to the emergence of a strong revolutionary movement lay in the lack of a clear sense of direction such as might have been provided by an inspiring ideology and an articulate leadership. One reason for this was doubtless the strength of the authorities. The vulnerability of the press to prosecution would have made it very difficult for a revolutionary ideology to be developed and diffused; and in so far as ideas did circulate about what a revolution might achieve, they seem to have remained extremely vague. There was talk of setting up a provisional government, of 'wiping off' the National Debt, and sometimes of repartitioning the land; but (except in a few Spencean publications which had a very limited sale) there was no clearly defined set of general objectives, no vision of an alternative society for which people might have felt impelled to risk their lives. As for leadership, the most conspicuous and influential figures in the national reform movement, in spite of their rhetoric about resistance, never saw themselves as revolutionaries. Hunt, after Peterloo, was intent on extracting *moral* capital from the event, and wished to put the authorities more conspicuously in the wrong through bringing actions against them in the courts. He opposed the plan of Watson and Thistlewood for the staging of simultaneous protest meetings as a means of mobilizing the people in massive numbers; and all he was prepared to recommend in the way of practical action was abstinence from goods subject to the excise tax.

The leading journalists, likewise, did not on the whole set a revolutionary tone. Papers such as Cobbett's *Register* and the *Black Dwarf* (particularly the latter, after Cobbett's flight to America in 1817) did play a central part in co-ordinating the public reform movement. They acquired a national circulation such as no radical paper of the 1790s had achieved, and by disseminating ideas and reports of meetings they gave radicals all over the country a sense of participation in a widespread campaign. But the characteristic style of the radical press in the Regency period was more satirical than violent. This may have been due partly to the fact that humour was difficult to prosecute: as was demonstrated in 1817 when William Hone, charged with blasphemous libel for publishing political parodies of the Catechism and the Creed, was triumphantly acquitted after a hilarious set of trials. Ridicule was a means of disarming the authorities, and contributed to a widespread undermining of deference. Yet, sharp though some of the humour was, it may to some extent have disarmed the radicals as well, in that laughter is hard to combine with the grim implacability that one associates with a revolutionary mentality. It is true that in 1819 a new batch of papers appeared in London – including the *Medusa*, the *Democratic Recorder*, and the *Cap of Liberty* – which had a more fiercely aggressive style. But none of this batch except the *Republican* (successor to *Sherwin's Weekly Political Register*) lasted for more than a few months, and the phase of intense indignation which succeeded Peterloo gave way in 1820 to the orgy of satire which marked the agitation relating to Queen Caroline.

George IV's attempt to divorce his consort provoked the most extensive anti-ministerial movement of the post-war period. The cause of the 'injured queen', assailed by an unpopular monarch and his unpopular ministers, was a cause with which anyone who was critical of the country's rulers could identify, and it attracted support from people of all types and classes: Whig peers, City radicals, Manchester artisans, rural labourers. In spite of the 'Six Acts' of December 1819, large demonstrations were held and the press was extremely outspoken. The government could not take action to suppress the agitation, partly because support for a member of the royal family could hardly be represented as seditious, and partly because of the ubiquity of public feeling. At the same time, however, the personalized, theatrical, at times almost saturnalian, nature of the affair meant that although the agitation was larger in scale it had less edge and substance than the working-class reform movement of the preceding years. Bootle Wilbraham, a Yorkshire landowner and MP, wrote in September 1820: 'Radicalism has taken the shape of affection for the Queen, and has deserted its old form, for we are all as quiet as lambs in this part of England, and you would not imagine that this had been a disturbed county twelve months ago.' When in November the government gave way and abandoned the proceedings against the queen, it was a notable triumph for public opinion. But the success was a transient one, and more gains probably accrued to the Whigs than to anyone else. Lord John Russell certainly believed that 'the Queen business had done a great deal of good in renewing the old and natural alliance between the Whigs and the people'. (New, 1961, p. 261; Stevenson, 1977, p. 141.)

Ideological Developments in the 1820s

After 1820 a number of factors combined to dampen radical agitation. One, probably the most important, was a markedly improved economic climate, which lasted – apart from a sharp recession in 1826 – until towards the end of the decade. Another was repression. The temporary immunity provided by the queen's affair did not interfere with the trials of leading radicals for alleged libels and acts of sedition committed in 1819; Carlile, Hunt, Knight, Bamford, Wooler and even Burdett were among those who suffered terms of imprisonment. And even more efficacious than prison sentences in reducing the strength and influence of the radical press was the Publications Act of 1819 (one of the Six Acts), which imposed a stamp duty of 4d. on all periodicals with any political content which were published more frequently than once a month and sold for less than 6d. Radicalism in the broad sense did not by any means die out in the 1820s, but it became rather disjointed, with a variety of lines being pursued by different people. Hunt tried to reanimate the campaign for universal suffrage, launching in 1821 his Great Northern Union, whose principal aim was to raise enough money to get some genuine representatives of the common people elected to parliament. Others felt that, conditions being unfavourable to popular agitation, it was an appropriate time to focus on doctrinal matters and to strive for a purification of radical ideology. Carlile, in particular, tried to secure wider acceptance of his own set of Painite principles. These included a commitment to republicanism and a rejection of the idea that all that was necessary was a restoration or renovation of the constitution through a radical reform of the House of Commons. Cobbett had always held firm to this idea, and he wrote in his *Political Register* on 13 November 1819: 'If we stick to our *one, legal, reasonable* object, we succeed: if we do not, we fail. The man, who, under the present circumstances, would propose *republicanism* as the ultimate object, must be nearly mad, or must have a desire to prevent any change at all.' But Carlile insisted that England had no constitution to renovate, and that the provision of a written one was a matter of high priority; and he argued that only an elective legislature and an elective executive could provide complete security against tyranny.

Carlile also insisted, even more forcibly, on the rejection of priestcraft and Christian superstition. There had been a significant free-thinking element in radical circles, especially in London, ever since Paine's *Age of Reason* was published in the 1790s; and it was for reprinting this work and other deist literature that Carlile was imprisoned for blasphemy in 1819. He not only attacked priests as 'black slugs' who lived off the labour of the industrious; he also maintained that they were as much a part of the machinery of oppression as the standing army: the priests controlled the minds of the people as the soldiers did their bodies, and it was vital to break this hold if political reform were to succeed. (Wiener, 1983, chapter 6.) Hunt firmly opposed both republicanism and infidelity, and a major controversy developed in the radical movement, especially over the issue of religion. There were strong feelings of anti-clericalism within the movement, hostility being directed not only against the clergy of the established Church but also against the Wesleyan ministry, which had done its best to deter members of Methodist congregations from participating in political agitation. There was also a distrust of evangelical religion in general, on the ground that its ardent emphasis on personal salvation distracted people from the possibilities of political improvement in this world. Yet there were many among the radicals who belonged to breakaway Methodist sects and other churches, and the numbers who rejected Christianity altogether seems to have been relatively small. The same could be said of the numbers who embraced republicanism (though it is worth mentioning in passing that Major Cartwright did so at the end of his life, asserting in *The English Constitution Produced and Illustrated* in 1823 that the Anglo-Saxon polity had included an elected monarch and no house of peers). In the conflict between the followers of Hunt and those of Carlile, the latter had the upper hand in some places such as Stockport, and in a number of towns Zetetic Societies were formed with Carlile's encouragement by groups interested in self-education and free thought. But for the most part the Huntites retained a predominance, although the Great Northern Union never achieved the mass membership that Hunt had hoped for. (Belchem, 1985, chapter 5.)

There were other developments in the 1820s which were important for the working-class movement, while being less immediately relevant than the Hunt–Carlile conflict to the issue of reform. In particular, this decade was a notable one in the evolution of socialist and anti-capitalist theories. (N.W. Thompson, 1984, chapters 2 and 5.) Hitherto there had been several different ways of explaining popular distress. Some contemporaries saw it as due to the breakdown of long-standing customs or regulations which had governed the relations between masters and workmen and preserved a healthy balance between their respective interests; but this kind of explanation seemed to account for the troubles of only a limited number of traditional trades. There were other analyses which focused on the expropriation of the people from the land, but these also seemed (in some eyes, at least) to have a limited application at a time when it was evident that manufacturing industry was constituting an ever-increasing proportion of the nation's productive resources. Thirdly, there were explanations which put the blame on political factors. We have seen that arguments about the burden of taxation were very commonly used in the post-war period. Somewhat later, especially after the government's decision in 1819 to return to cash payments, attention shifted to another politically determined factor, the manipulation of the currency. According to the analysis popularized by Cobbett, the 'paper money system', introduced when convertibility of notes into gold was suspended in 1797, had given rise to inflation; in order to facilitate the return to cash payments it was necessary to reduce the amount of paper money in circulation; and this deflation had a depressive effect on the economy and entailed a great increase in the real burden of the National Debt, most of which had been contracted in an inflated paper currency. This analysis had a considerable vogue in the early 1820s, and even had a wide attraction for members of the agricultural interest who were suffering from a sharp fall in prices. But it lost some of its credibility when in 1823 the resumption of cash payments was fully implemented without Cobbett's dire predictions of financial disaster being fulfilled.

The new socialist and anti-capitalist writers attributed impoverishment and exploitation not principally to government policies but to processes that were endemic to the economy: although, as we shall see, some recognized that economic exploitation was made possible by the legal system within which these processes operated. Robert Owen, who started propounding his schemes for co-operative communities around 1817, was more hostile towards competition than he was towards capital. It was competition in his view which held back the growth of prosperity and caused crises of overproduction such as occurred in the post-war period. It did so by forcing each employer to keep his wage-costs as low as possible, and by forcing workers to bid down wages in competing for jobs, with the result that the labouring classes in general were poorly remunerated and effective demand was prevented from increasing at the same rate as industrial production. Also, the Owenite analysis emphasized the role of competition in causing an over-rapid introduction of machinery and producing technological unemployment. The solution was to establish, on a community basis, a collectively organized system of production and exchange and a currency in which labour would constitute the standard of value. These arrangements would make possible full employment, and would ensure that each person's remuneration corresponded much more closely to the value of what he produced, with the result that consumption would be able to keep pace with rising output. Capitalists, Owen thought, need not be eradicated: indeed their capital might help to start co-operative communities and, despite the higher reward assigned to labour, their profits would rise rather than fall in consequence of the unleashing of the forces of growth.

Some other writers of the 1820s were much more critical of the capitalist and his profits. This was particularly true of Thomas Hodgskin, who wrote in 1820: 'Capital is the produce of labour,

41

and profit is nothing but a portion of that produce, uncharitably exacted for permitting the labourer to consume a part of what he has himself produced.' His theories were subsequently elaborated in three books, *Labour Defended against the Claims of Capital* (1825), *Popular Political Economy* (1827), and *The Natural and Artificial Right of Property Contrasted* (1832). In his view, the share of the produce of labour which went to the capitalist as unearned income under the name of profit was no more justifiable than the share which went to the landlord under the name of rent. The propertied classes had been able to secure and maintain, originally by naked force but latterly by their control over the making and enforcement of laws, a monopolistic hold over land and capital. In this situation the labouring class was obliged to work for the propertied classes on the latter's terms in order to obtain its livelihood, and the propertied classes were able to appropriate the whole of what the labouring class produced beyond what they allowed it for its own subsistence. Hodgskin also maintained that, with the growth in the scale and productivity of the non-agricultural sectors of the economy, the capitalists had taken over from the landowners the dominant position in the economic system and had become the principal exploiters of labour; in his words, they 'have long since reduced the ancient tyrant of the soil to comparative insignificance, while they have inherited his power over all the labouring classes'. In challenging the system and the doctrines that were used to justify it, Hodgskin put forward a theory of natural value and a theory of natural right. According to the former, nature provides man with a given object in return for a certain quantity of labour, and the natural price of an object is thus the quantity of labour required to produce it. According to the latter, every man has a natural right to the produce of his own labour: 'Nature bestows on every individual what his labour produces, just as she gives him his own body.' Hodgskin's theories provided a forceful critique of capitalism and of the injustices and oppressiveness which many people were coming to associate with it. He was not, however, a socialist. He did not favour collectivism in social and economic organization, as he believed that individualism was far more in accord with man's natural instincts. He said in defining his conception of the 'natural' right of property: 'The use of such things, like the making of them, must be individual, not common, selfish, not general ... It is the right of each individual to own for his separate and selfish use whatever he can make.' (Halévy, 1956, chapter 2.)

42

The ideas of Owen, Hodgskin and other critics of economic orthodoxy were attracting some attention in the popular newspapers of the 1820s, but at this period defences of orthodox political economy were also appearing in this section of the press. Francis Place was responsible for a number of such articles, which he wrote for the *Trades' Newspaper*, the *Bolton Chronicle* and other papers. He was an unusual person in that he had one foot in the working-class movement and one in Benthamite circles. He had come under the influence of Bentham and James Mill in the 1810s, and as well as absorbing Utilitarian political theory he had developed a deep respect for the doctrines of the political economists. Indeed he wrote in 1822 that it was 'impossible that the condition of the people can be greatly improved by those who do not themselves possess a competent knowledge of this, "the latest discovered science"'. (Thomas, 1962, p. 64.) He was anxious, therefore, to combat anti-capitalist ideas, which he regarded as delusive and as potentially damaging to working-class as well as middle-class interests. He was not as pessimistic as some followers of Malthus who held that the pressure of population growth was an almost insuperable obstacle to the improvement of working-class conditions. But he did believe that what basically determined the level of wages was the ratio of capital to population; and he maintained that working men could best advance their own long-term interests by limiting the increase of their numbers (he was bold enough to recommend artificial means of birth control for this purpose) and by doing nothing to hinder a high rate of capital accumulation. He considered that interventionist measures such as attempts to fix minimum wages were bound to do more harm than good, and he did not even believe that trade union activity could do much to improve the remuneration of working men.

It is somewhat ironic, therefore, that Place should have been the individual most responsible for what seems in retrospect the most notable landmark of the 1820s in labour history: the repeal of the combination laws in 1824. He campaigned for this on the grounds that the laws were an unjustifiable interference which poisoned relations between employers and employed and made trade unions secretive and violent. Another person who was campaigning for repeal at the same time, the framework-knitters' leader Gravener Henson, wished to replace the combination laws by an elaborate statutory machinery for regulating wages and other aspects of industrial relations. But Place, in alliance with the radical MP Joseph Hume, was able to get his policy of simple repeal carried through. In spite of this success, however, Place's economic ideas – or those he was trying to popularize – encountered strong opposition; and by the late 1820s the doctrines of the political economists, especially those of Malthus, were almost universally censured in the popular radical press. Also, in practical terms, Place's insistence that the only truly effective way to improve working-class conditions was to restrict the growth of population did not offer much prospect of amelioration in the short term, and working men understandably looked to other methods of advancing or protecting their interests. The 1820s saw a strengthening of trade unionism and inter-trade alliances, helped after 1824 by the emergence of a legal trade-union press. In addition, there were experiments in the setting up of co-operative institutions, both for consumers and for producers. Meanwhile, Hunt did his best to reactivate the popular movement for political reform, but had little success until the sharp deterioration in the economic situation at the end of the decade. Both he and Cobbett, while concerned about working-class conditions, were unreceptive if not hostile to Owenite and Hodgskinite ideas; and although one of the new writers, William Thompson, combined a belief in co-operative socialism with a belief in democracy, in general socialist and anti-capitalist theories had little impact on the parliamentary reform movement until the 1830s. (Prothero, 1979, chapters 9–13; Belchem, 1985, chapter 6.)

3 The Reform Bill Crisis 1829–32

The course of events in 1829–32 being somewhat complex, it may be helpful to provide at the outset a factual outline of the events leading up to reform, before considering the measure itself and the intentions and ideas that lay behind it. The period after the resignation of Liverpool in 1827 was one of confusion in ministerial politics, and saw the development of serious divisions in what was coming to be known as the 'Tory' party. The Duke of Wellington's ministry (1828–30) first alienated the liberal or Canningite Tories by refusing to countenance the transfer of East Retford's seats to Birmingham, and then alienated many Ultra-Tory devotees of the established Church by conceding Catholic Emancipation in April 1829. Some of the Ultras went so far as to announce their conversion to parliamentary reform, on the grounds that a House of Commons which truly represented opinion in the country would never have agreed to Emancipation; and in February 1830 the Tory Marquess of Blandford actually proposed a wide-ranging scheme of reform including the abolition of rotten boroughs, the exclusion of placemen from the Commons and the introduction of household suffrage. The settlement of the Catholic question may simultaneously have removed some Whig inhibitions about reform, inhibitions grounded on the fear that an extension of the franchise would give more leverage to popular anti-Catholicism; and the success of O'Connell's Catholic Association in extorting emancipation through organizational strength and extra-parliamentary agitation encouraged radicals to believe that political reform could be achieved by similar means. Meanwhile, a severe economic recession in 1829–30 caused widespread discontent in both rural and urban areas. In January 1830 the Birmingham Political

Union – the first of a number of such unions – was launched by Thomas Attwood to press for parliamentary reform; and this was also demanded, along with economy and reduced taxation, by several county meetings which took place in the early months of the year.

At the general election held in July–August 1830 after the death of George IV, there were notable manifestations of opposition to traditional modes of electoral management and patronage and, as very rarely happened at general elections under the unreformed system, the government failed to strengthen its position in the Commons. The July Revolution in Paris, though it occurred too late to have much effect on the election, stimulated reform sentiment in the country, and in the summer and autumn a contagious series of agricultural disturbances in the southern counties – the 'Captain Swing' riots – helped to create a very unsettled atmosphere. When parliament met in November, Wellington tried to rally his supporters by making an uncompromising speech against reform, but he only succeeded in uniting his opponents, and his government fell soon afterwards. It was followed by a ministry headed by Lord Grey, which was largely Whig but included several Canningites and one Ultra-Tory reformer. In December a committee of ministers was appointed to prepare reform proposals, and in March 1831 Lord John Russell introduced the Reform Bill in the House of Commons. In one of the most dramatic scenes in parliamentary history, it was passed on its second reading by a single vote. However, it was then amended in committee against the wishes of the government, and parliament was again dissolved. The general election of April–May 1831 resulted in a much increased Whig majority, and when the Bill was reintroduced it passed its second reading in July by a majority of 136, only to be rejected by the House of Lords in October. The rejection provoked a great outcry in the country, with serious riots in Bristol and elsewhere. In December a fresh Bill was introduced, with only slight modifications, and duly passed through the Commons; but there was again resistance in the Lords. As a result Grey resigned in May 1832, and in very tense circumstances Wellington tried, but failed, to form a government with the intention of undertaking a more moderate measure of reform. Grey returned to office, and persuaded William IV to threaten the creation of new peers if the Lords persisted in obstructing the Whig Bill. The Tory peers eventually gave way, and the Bill passed into law in June.

The Act as finally passed was not greatly different from the original Bill introduced fifteen months earlier. It was not as radical as the separate Reform Act which was passed for Scotland, for there the franchise had been very restricted in counties as well as boroughs, and the Act of 1832 increased the total electorate from 4,500 to 65,000. The Reform Act (England and Wales) was distinctly radical in some respects, but of rather conservative tendency in others. The feature of it which most surprised contemporaries was the drastic nature of the assault on pocket boroughs. Fifty-six boroughs which had returned two members each – most of them small boroughs in the south – lost their representation completely, and thirty more had their representation reduced from two seats to one. The extent of private parliamentary patronage had, of course, been one of the aspects of the old system which was most open to criticism; the Society of the Friends of the People, in its famous petition for reform presented by Grey in 1793, had maintained that 157 seats were demonstrably controlled by individual patrons and that almost as many more were subject to the 'influence' of powerful individuals. But within the ruling class such patronage had come to be widely regarded almost as a form of property, and few people had anticipated that the extremely aristocratic Whig cabinet would undertake disfranchisement on this scale. When Russell read out the original list of the boroughs to be eliminated, it caused what one observer called 'an absolutely electrifying shock'. (Brock, 1973, p. 161.)

Of the seats made available for redistribution in England and Wales, almost exactly half were given to towns which had not previously returned members. Twenty-two new boroughs (fourteen of them towns in the north and midlands) were assigned two members each, and twenty were given one member each. These provisions, though the number of seats involved formed only a segment of the House, were a significant offering to new urban interests. Several countervailing features of the Act should be noted, however. For one thing, it left in existence as parliamentary boroughs many country towns which belonged much more to the rural than to the urban sector of society; and this rural connection was strengthened by the fact that a large proportion of such boroughs (about half of them) had their constituency boundaries substantially extended into the surrounding countryside in order to raise their electorates to a respectable total. It should also be noted that while half the redistributed seats were given to new boroughs, the other half were devoted to increasing the representation of the counties. An increase in the number of county members had long been advocated by moderate reformers such as Christopher Wyvill, who had wanted to effect a shift of power from the Court and the borough patrons to the independent landed gentry, and in 1830–1 'country' elements similar to those which had mounted the Association Movement of the early 1780s had played an important part in the agitation for reform.

There were two other respects, though less important ones, in which the clauses affecting the distribution of seats brought some benefit to the landowning class. First, the fact that twenty-five of the larger counties were divided in two, each division returning two members, meant that these more compact constituencies could be more easily managed by the prominent landowners of the localities concerned. Secondly, the Act gave the county constituencies a more exclusively rural character than they had had before 1832. In some counties the growth of large industrial and commercial towns in the late eighteenth and early nineteenth centuries had meant that urban interests became a factor of increasing importance in county politics. In 1832, urban centres which had not previously had representation of their own (such as Birmingham, Manchester, Leeds and Sheffield) became borough constituencies. At the same time it was laid down by the borough freeholder clause that a piece of property which entitled a man to vote in a borough should not also give him the right to vote in the county. The boroughs were not altogether excised from the county constituencies, because the owner of a forty-shilling freehold within the boundaries of a borough, if his property did not qualify him for the borough vote as a £10 householder, was entitled to vote in the county. But it was certainly the case that the Act reduced the importance of urban interests in county constituencies and put the latter more firmly under the control of the landowning class.

In the Act's main provisions concerning the franchise, the most important changes related to the boroughs. A uniform qualification, enfranchising all males who occupied (as owners or tenants) houses worth £10 a year and paid their own rates, replaced the variety of franchises which had previously existed; and this gave the vote to large numbers of shopkeepers and other lower middle-class townspeople. In the counties, the basis of the electorate remained the forty-shilling freeholders, though they

48

were reinforced by other holders of property such as £10 copy-holders and long-leaseholders. In addition, under a clause introduced, against the wishes of the government, by Lord Chandos, the vote was extended to tenants-at-will who paid £50 or more in annual rent. This clause enfranchised a class of farmers who, because they had no security of tenure, were particularly dependent on their landlords.

From the point of view of the preservation of aristocratic influence over elections, perhaps the most important aspect of the Bill was the omission of something which it might have contained: the ballot. Secret voting had for some time been one of the major demands of the reform movement, and the ministerial committee of four which prepared the Reform Bill recommended its introduction: Lord Durham, who acted as chairman of the committee, was strongly in favour of it. However, Grey and a majority of the cabinet firmly prevented its inclusion.

The Motives of the Whigs

We come now to the question of what motives and intentions were in the minds of the Whig politicians who were responsible for carrying the Bill. There are several different ways of interpreting their motivation, and there may be a certain amount of truth in each of them. One of them emphasizes how much the Whig party stood to gain – and did actually gain – from reform. For nearly fifty years before 1830 this party had been continuously out of office, except for a brief participation in a coalition ministry in 1806–7 and an even briefer and more partial one in Canning's ministry of 1827; and there is evidence (some of which has been cited above) that a number of Whig politicians had been converted to parliamentary reform, notably in the period around 1820, by a realization that without such a reform they had little chance of getting back into power, or at least of staying in power if they did get back. While some aristocratic Whig families had a private stake in the unreformed system, it was clear in the early nineteenth century that their opponents had a much larger share of the pocket boroughs: it was estimated by the Tory J.W. Croker in 1827 that the Tory aristocracy controlled 203 nomination seats and the Whigs only 73. (Brock, 1973, p. 36.) So the Whigs as a party had no reason to be attached to the unreformed system, and indeed had good reasons for wishing it to be reconstructed. As for the effects of the reconstruction that actually took place, the diarist Charles

Greville said of the first parliament elected after the Reform Act: 'A Reformed Parliament turns out to be very much like every other Parliament ... except that the Whigs have got possession of the power which the Tories have lost.' (Woolley, 1938, p. 261.) Disraeli, in his *Vindication of the English Constitution* (1835), called the Reform Bill a Whig *coup d'état*, and he subsequently described the borough electorate created in 1832 as 'essentially, and purposely, a dissenting and low Whig constituency'. (Gash, 1953, p. 20.) In his view the £10 householders, among whom religious nonconformity was strong, formed a class which could be expected to vote predominantly Whig, and the Whig ministers had been fully aware of this. As to how much truth there is in this analysis, direct evidence that the Whig ministers had party political considerations in mind is hard to find, either in their speeches (where one would not expect to find it) or in their private correspondence. Also, one has to remember that the cabinet was not by any means exclusively Whig, and that it consisted almost without exception of aristocrats rather than 'careerists'. Indeed some of its members, such as Lord Althorp (Leader of the House of Commons) and Lord Grey himself, had the reputation of being reluctant politicians. Nevertheless, while it would carry little conviction to level a general charge of opportunism against the Whig leaders, it is hard to believe that they were altogether blind to considerations of party advantage; and it is perhaps worth noting that a member of Grey's own government, Sir John Cam Hobhouse, recorded his impression in February 1832 that Grey looked upon reform as 'a mere trick of state for the preservation of power'. (British Library Add. MSS 56556, f. 63.)

A quite different interpretation of the passage of the Bill, and one frequently put forward by the Whigs themselves, was that they were compelled to pass it by the pressure of public demand and the threat of revolution. Obviously, the argument that reform was necessary to prevent revolution was a very useful one for persuading parliament and the king to accept reform. But how far, one may ask, were the Whigs really acting under duress? It can be argued, on the one hand, that in the six years after 1823 there had not been a single petition to parliament in favour of reform; that even in 1830, although urban and rural recession had produced a strong demand for economy, there was no overwhelming pressure for reform of parliament; and that the Whigs themselves, needing some major cause to promote after the passage of Catholic Emancipation, did much to erect it into the great issue of the day. Brougham, in the flush of being returned as MP for Yorkshire at the general election, announced that he would take the initiative in pushing the question forward; and at a party meeting at Althorp's house before the new parliament met it was agreed that parliamentary reform should be treated, alongside retrenchment, as one of the party's 'great objects'. (A. Mitchell, 1967, pp. 236–43.) On the other hand, it can be argued that in the autumn of 1830 – although the agricultural rioting in the south and the simultaneous strike movement in the north west may have had little direct connection with political radicalism – the country did seem to many people to be in a restive and alarming state, especially in view of what had recently happened in France. It can also be argued that Wellington's unequivocal declaration *against* reform did far more than any Whig statements in its favour to excite public feeling over the issue, and that no government formed in November 1830 could have avoided tackling it in some way. Holland wrote in a letter of that month: 'Nothing but the adoption of the principle [of parliamentary reform] could I believe save our Monarchy or any of our institutions from destruction and confusion.' Moreover, from the years 1831–2 there is plenty of evidence, not only in parliamentary speeches and in Grey's correspondence with the king but also in private diaries and reports of confidential cabinet discussions, that ministers regarded civil war and revolution as real possibilities. (L. Mitchell, 1980, p. 81.)

A third interpretation, which has been put forward by D. C. Moore, argues that the Whig reform of parliament was not so much a concession to public pressure as an attempt to cure certain deficiencies in the unreformed system which had been impairing its credit and stability and making it less than satisfactory from the point of view of the governing class. He maintains, for instance, that the abolition of many decayed boroughs and the increase in the number of county members were intended to produce a strengthening of the legitimate influence of the landed classes over elections and a corresponding reduction of influences whose legitimacy was questionable. Legitimate influence derived from the leadership of homogeneous local communities such as landed estates; illegitimate influence was derived from cruder and less reputable sources and gave political power to people whose possession of it 'strained the ties of deference'. Moore also argues that one of the chief problems which the Reform Act was intended to cure was the destabilizing competition which had developed between rural and urban interests as a result of the incursion of the latter into many county constituencies. He puts special emphasis on the borough freeholder clause, which he interprets as an attempt to minimize such overlaps and collisions; and he holds that the Whigs were basically concerned to restructure the electoral system so that it was more securely based on hierarchical local communities in which traditional modes of influence and social discipline could operate effectively. Moore's interpretation has met with a considerable amount of criticism. It has been pointed out that the number of county constituencies in which substantial urban penetration took place before 1832 was quite small, and that the speeches and correspondence of the Whig ministers contain little evidence that the restriction of such penetration was one of their main objectives. Moore seems to have tied his analysis too closely to a particular aspect of the measure which was less important than he suggests; and in general he underplays the extent to which the government's policy was affected by public pressure. However, there is doubtless a considerable amount of truth in his point that the Reform Bill was a means whereby the landowning classes adapted the political structure in such a way as to 'perpetuate their own power while placating their social rivals'. (Moore, 1966, p. 58; Cannon, 1973; Moore, 1976, chapter 11.)

A fourth possible interpretation is that the Whig ministers – or at least some influential ones – were motivated not primarily by party interest, or fear of revolution, or class interest, but rather by a 'spirit of reform', a positive belief that reform was desirable and in accordance with Whig principles. The ministry included a number of people who had been committed reformers for some time. Certain Whig aristocrats such as Althorp and Russell saw it as their role to preside over a characteristically English process of ordered improvement and adaptation to social change, and they shared with ministers from professional backgrounds, such as Brougham and Jeffrey, a long-standing conviction that the electoral system was inadequate. They wished to purify it by removing the rotten boroughs and the corrupt practices associated with them. Also, they were genuinely concerned about the ever-increasing disharmony between the distribution of seats and the distribution of wealth and population, and they accepted that according to the very theory of the representation of interests which Mackintosh had expounded when arguing *against* radical reform in 1818, a change in the system was required to give more weight to industry and commerce. Russell, speaking in the Commons on 7 March 1831, recalled that what had converted him to the need for an extensive reform of parliament in 1822 had been his realization that 'the middle class, as compared with the corresponding body in the preceding century, had risen in wealth, and intelligence, and knowledge, and influence'. The many eulogistic remarks about the middle classes that were made by Whig speakers during the debates of 1831–2 may have contained an element of rhetoric, but behind them there was doubtless a real belief that the claims of these classes to a greater share of political power were incontestable. However, one feels that very few Whig ministers would have seen the Bill in such progressive terms as Althorp did when he wrote in a private letter in March 1831: 'The great principle of the measure is that henceforward there will be no privileged class and the power of the country being placed in the hands of the intelligence of the country, we may be satisfied that any improvements which may hereafter be required may be easily made.' (Wasson, 1980, p. 169.)

As between the various interpretations of Whig motivation, it is difficult if not impossible to say where the balance of truth lies. Different members of the government viewed the Bill in different ways, and many of them must have acted from a mixture of motives which even they would have found it hard to disentangle. None the less, some general points about the character and purposes of the Bill can be offered by way of conclusion to this discussion. One point is that the Bill put forward in March 1831 was much more radical than any of the Whig schemes mooted in the preceding years, and that although one or two people such as Durham would have liked it to be more radical still, it was probably more far-reaching than most ministers would have spontaneously wished. Yet it cannot be said that they were *forced* to produce the kind of measure they actually introduced, for the nature of the demand for reform as expressed in the numerous petitions presented in the winter of 1830–1 was generalized and indefinite, and hardly anyone *expected* the ministers to go as far as they did. As Place put it, 'the reformers, the enemies of reform, and the boroughmongers, were all equally surprised – and all for the same reason, namely, that the plan of reform had been made so extensive'. (Wallas, 1925, p. 258.)

The Bill was very much the product of the judgement of the Whig leaders, and there are several considerations which help to explain why they opted for a far-reaching measure. For one thing, the state of public opinion was such that only a measure of this kind seemed likely to arouse enthusiasm outside parliament; and although they hoped to be able to get the Bill passed without a further general election, ministers must have been aware that if it were held up an appeal to the country might be necessary. Also they doubtless calculated that something in the nature of a pre-emptive strategy offered the best chance of stability in both the short and the longer term. Several revolutions had been carried out in continental Europe by discontented middle-class groups with popular backing; and there were fears that if the committed but relatively moderate reformers who led bodies like the Birmingham Political Union were not satisfied, they would either become revolutionaries themselves, or lose control of the agitation to men whose methods and objectives were more extreme. In the longer perspective, a far-reaching measure seemed to be necessary to effect a settlement which, if not 'final' in the literal sense, would be likely to content the property-owning classes for the foreseeable future. In the debates on reform the Whigs were quite explicit about the need to placate the middle classes and attach them to the constitution, thereby separating them from the poorer classes and strengthening the forces of order.

There was one moment when the Whigs might have retreated to some extent from the line of policy adopted in the spring of 1831. In the following autumn, after the Lords' rejection of the Bill, some members of the government thought of modifying the measure in order to conciliate the moderate Tories; and William IV favoured this course as a means of resolving the dispute between the two Houses. But by that stage, middle-class opinion was even more attached to the Bill than the politicians who had initially brought it forward. The leaders of the political unions were insistent that the Bill should be reintroduced without being watered down, and at the same time the danger that extreme and unruly elements would gain ground if moderate reformers were unable to deliver the goods seemed actually to be materializing. Soon after the Bristol riots the Birmingham Political Union signalled its concern about this danger by discussing the possibility of reorganizing itself along military lines, 'to render the physical powers of the Union available for the preservation of life and property'; and the government was alarmed not only by the trend in popular agitation but also by the Union's plan to take the law into its own hands. Before the end of November ministers had put aside the idea of a compromise solution, and pressure from public opinion seems in this instance to have had an appreciable influence on their conduct. (Ferguson, 1960, pp. 268–70; Flick, 1978, pp. 68–9.) It is important to reiterate, however, that although the state of feeling in the country was a major factor in their deliberations throughout the Reform Bill crisis, at no stage did it force them into anything like a capitulation. Overall they gave a certain amount away, including a considerable number of Tory pocket boroughs; but there was no large-scale transfer of power from one class to another. The landed interest retained, and in some ways strengthened, its hold over the greater part of the electoral system, and the share of power allotted to middle-class interests was no more than a subordinate one.

The Middle Classes and the Bill

Compared with the attitudes of the Whigs towards the Reform Bill, the support given to it by middle-class reformers requires less in the way of explanation. We have seen that in the 1820s the idea of direct representation for new manufacturing and commercial interests had attracted widespread support in the great industrial towns. In that relatively peaceful decade even people of conservative instincts overcame their fear of the popular turbulence that parliamentary elections might cause in urban communities; and the frustration of what seemed quite unobjectionable schemes for the transfer of a few seats from corrupt boroughs to selected centres of wealth and population tended to fan the middle-class demand for increased representation. The basic grievance was expressed by the Birmingham Political Union at its inaugural meeting in January 1830: 'The landed interest, the church, the law, the monied interest, have *engrossed*, as it were, the House of Commons into their own hands ... *But the interests of industry and trade have scarcely any representatives at all!*' In earlier years, when a strong popular agitation for reform had arisen (as in the post-war period) the reaction of most owners of property had been a defensively negative one. But in 1830 this sort of reaction did not occur. The obdurate conservatism of Polignac was held responsible for the July Revolution in France, and a substantial reform seemed necessary in England in order to defuse a threatening situation and stabilize the country. Hobhouse wrote to Burdett in November: 'Every respectable householder is now a Reformer as the only means of saving his property.' (Bodleian Library, Oxford, MS Eng. letters, d.96, f.24.) The Whig plan, unfolded in the following March, seemed to satisfy middle-class needs very fully. It did, by its far-reaching nature, frighten off some of the urban 'Tories' who had previously shown an interest in restricted measures of redistribution, as it also frightened off most of the Ultra-Tory landowners who had flirted with parliamentary reform in the aftermath of Catholic Emancipation. But by the great bulk of middle-class people the Bill was welcomed as offering them at the same time an appropriate status within the political system and security against more democratic schemes. The *Manchester Courier*, one of the few provincial newspapers which opposed the Bill, lost half its circulation through doing so, and Grey was probably justified in telling the king's private secretary in November 1831 that the middle classes were 'activated by an intense and almost unanimous feeling in favour of the measure'. (Evans, 1983, p. 210.)

It should be noted, however, that behind this apparent unity there were considerable differences over the ulterior purposes for which reform of parliament was sought; and this underlying lack of consensus may help to explain why the urban bourgeoisie was not more assertive at this time and did not mount a more far-reaching challenge to aristocratic hegemony. The Birmingham Political Union, although it provided an organizational model that was used by many other towns, did not co-operate closely with political unions in other areas, and was ideologically separated from most of them by the distinctive views on economic policy that were associated with it. Attwood's principal aim, which antedated by many years his interest in parliamentary reform, was to secure a reform of the currency. He, like Cobbett, considered that the restoration of convertibility had had deflationary effects; but whereas Cobbett approved of the return to gold and simply wanted it to be accompanied by a scaling down of the National Debt and a reduction of taxation, Attwood believed that a controlled re-expansion of paper money was desirable in order to raise the level of demand, increase economic activity, and restore full employment. During the trade depression of 1829, Attwood organized a great Birmingham petition to parliament calling for currency reform, and it was when this evoked no response that he made reform of parliament his immediate goal and formed the Birmingham Political Union with the help of several businessmen who shared his economic ideas. In Manchester, parliamentary reform was linked to different objectives. Manufacturers and merchants in the cotton industry, being heavily dependent on the stability of international trade, wanted the currency left alone. What they sought was a repeal, or at least a modification, of the corn laws; agricultural protection, it was believed, handicapped exporting industries by keeping their wage-costs at an artificially high level, and made it difficult for foreign countries to sell grain to Britain and to purchase manufactured goods in return. Also, Manchester differed from Birmingham in that, whereas Attwood and a number of his chief associates came from Anglican and Tory backgrounds, the middle-class Mancunian reformers were predominantly Dissenters. This made Manchester more typical of English provincial cities, in several of which the campaign for parliamentary reform was an extension of local struggles with entrenched Anglican elites. (Briggs, 1952; Flick, 1978, pp. 12–13, 71–2.)

There was one branch of middle-class opinion which might well have been expected, because of the radicalism of its principles and aspirations, to be dissatisfied with the Reform Bill. The Benthamites had been committed to a programme of reform which included universal (or something approaching universal) suffrage, annual parliaments, and the ballot, and they had been outspokenly hostile to the aristocracy and to the Whig party. The *Westminster Review* had been founded to combat the views of the *Edinburgh* as well as the Tory *Quarterly*, and in its first number (January 1824) James Mill had criticized the Whig periodical for its efforts to 'gain favour from both the few and the many' by a system of 'trimming', which involved championing the interests of the aristocracy at one moment and those of the people at another. In 1829 the *Edinburgh* had gone on to the attack with a brilliant article, written by the young lawyer T.B. Macaulay, which exposed a number of weaknesses in the reasoning of Mill's *Essay on Government*; and the sharp debate provoked by this article had continued through several issues of the two reviews. In fact there was one important point on which Benthamites and Whigs were agreed: that for the sake of social peace and economic prosperity it was vital to preserve security of property. But they tended to disagree about which types of government were most inimical to such security. According to Mill, an irresponsible monarchy or aristocracy was the kind of regime most to be avoided, because it was certain to despoil the community it ruled over. In Macaulay's view, on the other hand, it was under a popular form of government that property was most likely to be endangered. Bentham had pointed to the experience of American states such as Pennsylvania to show that a more or less democratic electoral system could be combined with security of property; and Mill, who had a great faith in the power of reason and in the educability of the people at large, thought that the lower classes in England could be made to realize that they stood to lose much more than they stood to gain from an invasion of existing property rights. But Macaulay maintained that the American example was not relevant because property there was much more widely diffused than in Europe, and he held that in a society which had a large majority of poor men and a small minority of rich men it would be extremely difficult to persuade the poor that it was against their interest to redistribute wealth.

Even before the appearance of Macaulay's article in 1829 there had been some misgivings in the Utilitarian camp about how far full democracy was compatible with the preservation of private property. Ricardo, for instance, had written in 1818 that if there was reason to think that certain sections of society did not have a 'sacred regard' for the rights of property, those sections ought to be excluded from the franchise until they were properly enlightened. (Dinwiddy, 1978, p. 19.) The articulation of socialist ideas in the 1820s strengthened such misgivings, and helped to prepare the way for a tactical retreat by the Benthamites from the advanced position they had taken up on the reform question. Shortly before the unveiling of the Whig Reform Bill in 1831, George Grote published a pamphlet called *Essentials of Parliamentary Reform* in which he used a line of argument similar to the one sketched earlier by Ricardo. He did not admit that there was much real evidence of popular hostility towards the institution of private property; but he thought it would be permissible, as a means of 'allaying the apprehensions of the middle classes' and of ensuring that the franchise was not extended to the uneducated, to establish for the time being a pecuniary qualification, provided that this was low enough to produce a total electorate of at least a million voters. Meanwhile, a reform which gave predominance to the middling classes would remove the 'inveterate oligarchical taint' which infected the political system, and the poor, though unable to vote, would benefit from such things as a reduction of taxes and an amelioration of the legal system.

The Benthamites did not expect the aristocratic Whig government to propose a reform that would be really worth supporting. The young MP Charles Buller wrote in his pamphlet *On the Necessity of a Radical Reform* in February 1831: 'Without accusing the Government of a design of deceiving the people, there is good ground for apprehending that they will present us with a very inadequate plan.' A few weeks later, however, after the Whig measure had been made public, he wrote enthusiastically to Thomas Carlyle: 'This Bill is certainly a most capital measure – the destructive part at any rate being nobly bold.' (National Library of Scotland, MS 665, no. 31.) In several respects, of course, the Reform Bill did have serious deficiencies from a Utilitarian perspective. Its biggest shortcoming was the omission of the ballot, to which the Benthamites had attached special importance as the means of putting an end to the corruption and coercion of voters and providing real scope for popular choice; James Mill had gone so far as to say in a *Westminster* article of July 1830 that even if unaccompanied by other reforms the ballot would do much to remedy the defects of the constitution. Another weakness of the Reform Bill from his point of view was that it was largely based on a notion which he had explicitly rejected in his *Essay on Government*: that the electoral system should provide representation for interest groups rather than for the mass of the people. Mill had argued that under such a system the various groups or 'fraternities' represented would band together into a 'motley aristocracy' and would promote the interests they had in common at the expense of the community at large. None the less, the Bill did go much further than the Benthamites had expected, and far enough to win strong support from them.

Indeed, they have been credited by Joseph Hamburger (1963) with an important role in securing the Bill's passage. According to him, James Mill, in particular, was responsible for putting forward the idea that the only way to secure a substantial measure of reform was to intimidate the aristocracy by stimulating popular agitation to the point at which it *seemed* to be revolutionary; and Hamburger cites a letter of October 1831 in which Mill told Albany Fonblanque, editor of *The Examiner*: 'The people ... should appear to be ready and impatient to break out into action, without actually breaking out.' How influential Mill was in originating and diffusing this notion is questionable; but it is true that, just as arguments about the danger of revolution were used by the Whig ministers to put pressure on the king and the House of Lords, so they were used by middle-class agitators and journalists to alarm the ruling class and to keep the Whig ministers up to the mark. It is also true that some of the middle-class reformers who used this tactic, such as Francis Place and the Birmingham solicitor Joseph Parkes, were members of the Benthamite circle. Parkes had close contacts with the Birmingham Political Union, and Place was involved in founding, in the autumn of 1831, a National Political Union in London which was intended to unite middle- and working-class supporters of reform as the Birmingham Union had done. Also, both of them had channels of communication with the government: Place through Sir J.C. Hobhouse, MP for Westminster, and Parkes (who had Whig as well as Benthamite affiliations) through Althorp and Durham. In October–November 1831, and again during May 1832, they did their best to create the impression that the country was on the verge of revolution; and on the latter occasion they were ostensibly preparing for drastic moves, such as an organized run on the banks or even an armed insurrection, to be undertaken if Wellington took over the government or if the Whigs were denied the means of breaking the resistance of the Lords. Whether, if the Bill *had* been thwarted, some kind of direct action would have been initiated by middle-class leaders of the reform movement, one cannot say for certain. Some of them, such as Place, were heavily committed to pursuing a militant line of policy as far as it proved to be necessary. On the other hand most (if not all) of them would have been very unhappy about an actual resort to measures which might have produced widespread disorder and given a golden opportunity to extremists; and there is little evidence that the council of the Birmingham Political Union, which Place would have counted upon to give a lead to the country, had any real intention of raising the standard of revolt. As for the role of the Benthamites in helping to create the atmosphere of crisis which, both in the autumn of 1831 and in May 1832, made it difficult if not impossible for politicians to attempt the substitution of a more moderate reform policy for the original Bill, it may be that their contribution has been overrated owing to the fact that their papers – and especially Place's somewhat self-centred account of the episodes concerned – have survived and been much used by historians.

Working-Class Radicals and the Bill

There remains to be considered, in relation to the Reform Bill agitation, the question of the part played by working-class radicalism. The first point to be made here is that the years 1829–32 were years of intensive and varied working-class activity, in which the pursuit of political reform was only one strand. Other strands of agitation included trade unionism; the co-operative movement which, inspired partly by Owen's ideas and partly by the practical needs and experiments of working men, underwent a great expansion at this time; and the movement to secure a reduction of working hours in factories, which first achieved large-scale organization in the early 1830s. Although Owen and the Tory Richard Oastler, leaders respectively of the latter two movements, were actually hostile to radical agitation, these three strands of activity were not by any means incompatible with it. But political radicalism had to compete with them to some extent for attention, and it was not always given priority in working-class circles. For example, in the north west a great deal of energy was going into trade union action in 1829–30. After the failure of a massive strike in the cotton industry, John Doherty founded a national spinners' union in September 1829, and in the following year he built up a general union of trades, the National Association for the Protection of Labour (NAPL), which spread into the west midlands hosiery district and the Staffordshire potteries. Its principal aim was to prevent wage reductions, and at a general delegate meeting at Nottingham in March 1831 it was agreed that, to prevent the Association from being sidetracked into the reform controversy, a rule should be laid down excluding political subjects from its discussions. Doherty none the less stressed in his paper *The Voice of the People* (which had been set up with NAPL funds) that members of the Association as individuals should involve themselves in the struggle for political rights, and he himself devoted much space to it in his paper. He also developed, however, a strong commitment to co-operation and made an unsuccessful effort to inject new vitality into the NAPL, which had suffered a number of failures in attempts to support strikes, through involving it in the co-operative movement. Subsequently he transferred most of his energies to the movement for factory reform, becoming editor early in 1832 of a new paper, the *Poor Man's Advocate*, which was mainly devoted to this cause. On 9 July 1831, at the height of his enthusiasm for co-operation, a letter signed 'An Old Radical' appeared in Prentice's paper the *Manchester Times*, maintaining that Doherty was a man of 'no fixed principle' and urging radicals to 'give up scheming' and work together for political reform, after which 'all else will follow as a matter of course'. (Kirby and Musson, 1975, p. 331.) Another illustration of the diversity of the concerns of working-class activists is provided by the National Union of the Working Classes (NUWC), which for several years after its formation in the spring of 1831 was the most lively and extensive organization of its kind in London, and indeed in the country. Some of its membership was drawn from two different but overlapping bodies formed in 1829, the Radical Reform Association which had stood for traditional Huntite radicalism, and the British Association for Promoting Co-operative Knowledge. It also included Spenceans and free thinkers, expatriate Irishmen pressing for the repeal of the Union and radicals from the metropolitan parishes who had been agitating for democratically elected vestries and the abolition of church rates. The range of views and preoccupations represented made the NUWC a stimulating forum for debate, but it also limited its ability to campaign effectively for any particular object; and although the co-operators who were prominent in the organization tended to see co-operation and political reform as complementary rather than as conflicting alternatives, some radicals found the NUWC less helpful in regard to parliamentary reform than they had hoped. (Rowe, 1977, pp. 151–66.)

Obviously one reason why some working-class leaders showed a limited amount of interest in parliamentary reform at this time was the fact that the Whig Reform Bill offered nothing directly to people of their class. Indeed in a sense it offered worse than nothing, since under the unreformed system at least a few constituencies had had a genuinely democratic franchise, which was now being replaced by the uniform £10 householder qualification. Despite this fact, however, and the previous commitment of popular radicals to universal suffrage, annual parliaments and the ballot, the Reform Bill was so unexpectedly bold that the initial reaction of the leaders of radical opinion was overwhelmingly favourable. Cobbett, although two years earlier he had issued a joint declaration with Hunt saying that half a loaf was worse than no bread, greeted it enthusiastically; and so did Carlile, whose political views had moderated since the early 1820s. Only a few prominent figures – such as Hunt, who had been elected MP for Preston in December 1830, and the journalist Henry Hetherington – maintained from the start that it was totally inadequate, though they were subsequently joined by others in this opinion.

Between those who supported the Bill and those who opposed it there was fierce and vituperative debate. The former argued that the Bill should be seen as a stepping stone, a first instalment in the payment of a debt, a crucial breach in the prescriptive defences of the old system. The journalist William Carpenter wrote in October 1831: 'If the principle be once set of altering the constitution, the same arguments urged in favour of the first change will be irresistible when urged in favour of subsequent changes.' (Brock, 1973, p. 166.) Meanwhile Hunt, finding most of the London-based radical press against him, directed his message to the working classes in the north, through speeches at public meetings and a series of published *Addresses*. He denounced Cobbett and Carpenter as traitors, and employed – with much emphasis on his own consistency – the same arguments as he had used in the past in favour of universal suffrage and against moderate reform. He had maintained for years that working men deserved the vote as a matter of justice, and needed it in order to protect the fruits of their labour, principally against heavy and inequitable taxation. He said of the Reform Bill in a speech at Bolton in April 1831 that 'it certainly was all very good, very *liberal*; but *would it get the people something more to eat?*' (Belchem, 1985, p. 228.) In addition, he spent much time exposing and denouncing the selfishness of the Whigs' motives (anticipating, in fact, some of the interpretations discussed earlier in this chapter). He said that the Bill was intended to strengthen their hold on the power which had eluded them for so long, and that as a result of clauses which were being largely ignored by the press, such as the division of the counties, the influence of the aristocracy over elections would be increased rather than diminished. He also maintained – in the first speech he delivered after the Bill was introduced in the Commons on 2 March – that the Whigs' purpose seemed to be to extend the suffrage to the middle classes 'in order to prevent the lower classes from obtaining their rights'.

The other outstanding critic of the Bill on the radical side was Hetherington's paper *The Poor Man's Guardian*, started in July 1831. This was the most famous and successful of the 'unstamped' newspapers of the 1830s: papers which were cheap enough to be purchased by working men because they were published, in defiance of the law, without payment of the stamp duty imposed in 1819. The *Guardian* used many of the same arguments as Hunt, but gave a somewhat different flavour to its criticisms by incorporating elements of anti-capitalist analysis. In an editorial of 30 July 1831 on the Reform Bill, it asked whether kings and priests and lords were the only people who fattened in idleness on the labour of the people. 'Do not your "masters", your traders – from the banker and merchant down to the £10-a-year-coal-shed-keeper, – in fact from lord mayor down to "*middle man*" – do not they also enrich themselves at your expense?' Ideas drawn from Hodgskin and others about the exploitative nature of industrial and commercial profits were finding expression in some other papers as well, and in occasional debates of the NUWC. But in general radical critics of the Reform Bill did not express hostility towards the middle classes on the grounds that as capitalists or employers or 'middlemen' they were exploiting the workers; much more often, hostility towards them was based on the belief that they were being willingly drawn into an alliance with the aristocracy and a participation in its political privileges. (Rowe, 1977, pp. 152–6; Prothero, 1979, pp. 282–4.)

The balance, in working-class opinion, between those who favoured and those who opposed the Bill varied considerably from one area to another. In some places, a large majority of politically conscious working men co-operated with middle-class reformers in supporting it. Birmingham was the most notable example of such collaboration. A strong movement of artisan radicalism had occurred there in the post-war years, but lacking assistance from middle-class elements it had been vulnerable to attack from local loyalists and had been systematically crushed by prosecutions. When the agitation for reform revived in 1830, George Edmonds and others who had led the earlier movement were inclined to participate in the more broadly based one represented by the Birmingham Political Union, and were influential in obtaining artisan support for it. Other factors which helped the Union to secure and retain the backing of many working men were Attwood's leadership and the nature of his ideas. He acquired great personal prestige in Birmingham through his success in managing large public meetings, and through the sense of local pride generated by the conspicuous part which the Union played under his leadership in the national reform movement. Consequently, although there were some radicals in the town (and indeed in the council of the Birmingham Political Union) who wished to go further than Attwood on the reform question, there was little attempt to challenge his authority. On the ideological front, his explanation of economic depression and unemployment put the blame on mismanagement of the nation's finances and discounted the possibility of conflicts of interest between capitalists and workers. He said at a Birmingham town meeting on 13 December 1830 that the interests of masters and men were identical, and that they should go hand in hand to 'knock at the gates of the Government and demand the redress of their common grievances'. Moreover, according to an argument put forward some years ago by Asa Briggs in an important pair of articles (1948 and 1952), such ideas had a special cogency in Birmingham because the industrial structure of the town was not such as to produce wide divisions between social classes. There having been little displacement of skilled manual work by machinery, the characteristic unit of production in the metal trades was the small workshop rather than the factory, and although some large capitalists had emerged the distance between masters and journeymen was not usually very great. It has been pointed out in relation to Briggs's argument (Behagg, 1982) that the leaders of the Birmingham Political Union came from the wealthy business elite rather than from the small workshop sector of the economy, and that later in the 1830s they were to encounter strong opposition from working-class radicals. It has also been pointed out (Sykes, 1980) that a predominance of small-scale industrial firms was not always associated with a lack of popular militancy and class-consciousness. None the less the industrial context may go some way towards explaining the muted nature of class conflict in Birmingham at the time of the Reform Bill.

Sheffield, where the cutlery trade was largely organized on a workshop basis, was another town in which a single political union was able to rally local opinion behind it in support of the Bill; and the same thing happened in Coventry, where masters and journeymen had a common interest in securing protection for the local ribbon trade. But there were other places, such as Manchester and Leeds, where attempts to unite middle- and working-class reformers had much less success. In the Manchester area, social cleavages and class antagonisms were very pronounced. The ideology of the liberal merchants and manufacturers, based on a somewhat selective adoption of the ideas of the political economists, did resemble Attwood's in holding that the interests of employers and workmen were inseparable. The *Manchester Guardian* went so far as to say in April 1830: 'As the mass of the middle classes never can have any interests adverse to the happiness and prosperity of those below them in society, the rights of the humblest order would be quite safe from a constituency in which that mass had a preponderance.' (McCord, 1967, p. 378.) But major confrontations between spinners and millowners over wage reductions had given a hollow ring to such claims; and among handloom weavers there was deep resentment over the introduction of power-looms, resentment which had given rise to a fierce revival of machine-breaking in Lancashire in 1826. A Manchester Political Union set up on the Birmingham model by Archibald Prentice in the summer of 1830 proved to have little appeal for working men, and early in the following year the local Huntites founded a Political Union of the Working Classes (PUWC), to which the weavers in particular gave strong support as they had to Hunt's radicalism in 1819. In Leeds also, the rapid introduction of machinery and an accompanying expansion of the factory system accentuated class divisions, and produced great discontent among clothworkers who were having to cope with the transition from domestic industry to the mills. Indeed for working men in this area in the early 1830s conditions of work in factories tended to be the dominant issue, with Leeds becoming the centre of Oastler's 'short time' movement. Meanwhile, there was a strong middleclass agitation in support of the Reform Bill, headed by Edward Baines of the *Leeds Mercury*. But the fact that Baines and many of his associates were economic liberals who were lukewarm if not hostile towards factory legislation helped to limit the extent of working-class support for their views on parliamentary reform; and after a visit by Hunt in November 1831 a Radical Political Union was set up which declared both for universal suffrage and for a ten hours bill.

Although Hunt's ideas never won *general* support from the working classes, they did evoke favourable responses in several parts of the industrial north, and popular dissatisfaction with the Reform Bill, there and in London, was particularly apparent in the autumn of 1831. The period of uncertainty and excitement after the Bill's rejection by the Lords, when the intentions of the Whig ministry were still unclear, was an opportune time for those who were discontented with the measure to press for a more democratic one. A public meeting arranged on 10 October by the moderate reformers of Manchester to protest against the Bill's defeat was swamped by an influx of Huntite radicals under the leaders of the PUWC, who proposed and carried resolutions in favour of universal suffrage. The membership of the PUWC expanded rapidly, and new Huntite Unions were formed at Middleton and Ashton-under-Lyne as well as at Leeds. Meanwhile in London the NUWC underwent a similar expansion, and committed itself to even more extreme objectives such as the abolition of all hereditary ranks; and an open-air meeting which it called for 7 November seemed to the government so threatening that it was banned. However, once the reintroduction

66

of the Bill was announced, the ultra-radical agitation lost steam. The fact was that the Whigs had framed a measure that was sufficiently substantial to make it difficult for its left-wing critics to generate sustained opposition to it, at least when there seemed to be a fair prospect of its being passed; and it is significant that even Hunt was prepared to vote for the Bill in the House of Commons, on the grounds that the disfranchisement of the rotten boroughs was worth carrying out.

Also, the ultra-radicals could offer no strategy that was a credible alternative to the campaign for the Bill. There was some talk in late 1831 of simultaneous meetings and street-fighting, and William Benbow floated the idea of a general strike for political purposes: a 'grand national holiday' which would precipitate a collapse of the system and a total reform. But this idea, being clearly impracticable when popular opinion was divided, was rejected by the NUWC committee, and an attempt to hold a 'national convention' of Huntite radicals at Manchester in December was not a success. One further point is that the Whigs and moderate reformers were paradoxically assisted, during the Reform Bill crisis as a whole, by the fact that the Tory aristocracy put up such a stubborn resistance. This helped to divert popular attention from the limitations of the Bill and to focus it on the evils of oligarchy and boroughmongering and 'Old Corruption'. The riots at Nottingham and Bristol in October 1831, which were directed against prominent opponents of reform such as the Duke of Newcastle and Sir Charles Wetherell (Recorder of Bristol), can be seen as reflections of this orientation; and in May 1832 the renewed resistance of the Lords and the threat of a Wellington ministry produced an almost unanimous chorus of support for the Whig measure. Even in Manchester there was a temporary patching-up of differences; the PUWC agreed to endorse an address to the king drawn up by the moderate reformers on condition that the latter co-operated in forming a new Manchester Association to Promote Reform, which would not only back the Whig Bill but also seek further reform once it was passed. When, however, the news arrived that the Whigs were to stay in office, the moderates declared the formation of such an association to be 'unnecessary'. (Prothero, 1979, pp. 286–9; Sykes, 1982, pp. 363–78.)

4 The Aftermath of Reform

Whigs and Parliamentary Radicals in the 1830s

At the first general election held under the Reform Act in December 1832 the Whigs won a massive majority, and they were to remain in office, apart from a few months of minority Conservative government in the winter of 1834–5, until 1841. From one perspective this period of Whig rule – or at least the early part of it – can be seen as a notably progressive one, and this owed much to the new situation and expectations created by the reform of parliament. As has been indicated above, the electoral system was by no means completely transformed. Overall, there was less than a doubling of the electorate; the great majority of MPs, for boroughs as well as counties, continued to be members of landed families; about three-quarters of the borough constituencies had electorates of less than a thousand; some seventy seats remained in the control of individual patrons; and influence and bribery continued to be important factors in elections. None the less, over the system as a whole the number of 'open' constituencies had greatly increased, and there was a corresponding increase in the amount of attention that members and candidates had to pay to the opinions of electors. In addition the first elections under the new system aroused particular interest and excitement, and a large number of MPs came to Westminster pledged to pursue various reforms.

In the post-1832 period the Whig ministers did not head a coherent party, but in confrontation with the Tories they were generally supported by a medley of Whigs, Liberals and Radicals, as well as by a group of Irish MPs who followed the lead of O'Connell. As has been indicated above, very few members of the government which had passed the Reform Bill had welcomed it as a change that would open the way to other reforms. After 1832, however, they were almost bound to present it in this light because of the nature of the support which they had acquired in parliament and the country. Althorp said that the Whigs could only maintain their position by taking the lead in popular measures, and Grey said in the House of Lords (17 July 1833) that the Reform Act must be regarded as a prelude to other reforms which would 'give satisfaction to the country, and security to the Monarchy'. In the years 1833–5 there was an unprecedented spate of important legislation. The year 1833 saw the first state grant for educational purposes, the abolition of slavery in the British colonies (a measure strongly demanded by evangelical and Dissenting opinion), and the passage of Althorp's Factory Act, which restricted the working hours of children in textile factories and made certain compulsory provisions for their education. In 1834 the Poor Law Amendment Act was passed, and in 1835 the Municipal Corporations Act, both of them measures which introduced a degree of democratization into local government. The former removed the ancient system of poor relief which had been essentially based on the parish and managed by parish overseers and magistrates, and it created instead a network of larger units, the Poor Law Unions, in which the administration of relief was controlled by Boards of Guardians elected by the rate-payers. The latter act dissolved the old oligarchical town corporations, which had been predominantly Anglican and Tory, and replaced them with municipal councils elected by rate-paying householders. Coming on top of the repeal of the Test and Corporation Acts in 1828, this measure was particularly important in providing the nonconformist section of the middle classes with enlarged opportunities in local politics.

After 1835, there was less in the way of major legislation. The government was headed by the conservative-minded Lord Melbourne, and it had to face some obstruction from the Tory majority in the House of Lords. Lord John Russell was the most vigorous member of the government in its later years, and as Home Secretary between 1834 and 1839 he carried further the reforms of the criminal law and the penal system that Peel had initiated in the 1820s. He also tried to give the ministry a new lease of life by undertaking fresh initiatives in fields such as education, but had only limited success. On 'organic' or constitutional reform, he concurred with his Whig colleagues in adopting a generally negative stance; indeed, he earned the nickname 'Finality Jack' by firmly declaring in a speech of November 1837 that he would not countenance any alteration of the 1832 settlement. Though it is true that in 1839 he was instrumental in persuading the cabinet to make the ballot an 'open question', he recommended this move not because he himself had been converted to the ballot, but because many government supporters were in favour of it and the ministry needed to minimize friction with those on whose votes it depended.

Among those who usually supported the Whig governments of the post-1832 period there were many MPs who were prepared to vote for certain organic reforms. In 1833, 164 members voted for a motion for shorter parliaments; and, largely because of the bribery and intimidation which were very apparent at the general elections of the 1830s, motions for the ballot attracted steadily growing support during the decade, 106 members voting for it in 1833 and 216 in 1839. However, the number of MPs who were commonly classified as Radicals – the term being loosely applied at this time to those who gave high priority to organic reform – was smaller than these figures might suggest. There was no clear dividing line between Liberals and Radicals, but most estimates of the number of Radicals in the 1833 parliament lay between 50 and 100. The category was a miscellaneous one, which included Attwood and Joshua Scholefield, leaders of the Birmingham Political Union, and Dissenting manufacturers from the north west such as G.W. Wood (South Lancashire) and Joseph Brotherton (Salford). But the men who aspired to lead the Radical section in parliament were a small set of members who had no strong connection with urban or Dissenting interests: the so-called 'Philosophic Radicals'. They were able and highly articulate, and regarded Jeremy Bentham (who had died in 1832) and James Mill as their intellectual mentors. The group included George Grote, Sir William Molesworth, J.A. Roebuck and Charles Buller; it had a close ally of an older generation in Joseph Hume; and it had associates who were prominent outside parliament as writers, state servants or political activists, such as John Stuart Mill, Edwin Chadwick and Francis Place.

The Philosophic Radicals felt that the settlement of 1832 had left the aristocracy with far too much power, and that the Whigs, as a segment of the aristocracy, should be regarded with great suspicion. Indeed, in the parliament of 1833 they sat on the Opposition benches in the House of Commons; and for some time they had ambitious hopes of being able to bring about a realignment of parties. Their interpretation of the basic political situation was summed up by Roebuck in 1835: 'Former disputes and contests in politics were between various sections of the Aristocracy: the contest that is now going on is between the *Aristocracy* and the *People*.' (Hamburger, 1965, p. 62n.) According to this analysis, the current position of the Whigs was anomalous, and what the Philosophic Radicals hoped was that the mass of Liberals and Radicals could be detached from the Whig leadership to form a popular 'movement' party, while the Whigs shifted over to form a defensive alliance with the Tories (or Conservatives, as they were now coming to be called). In some ways such hopes were not unrealistic. On a number of occasions in the 1830s the Whig front bench was supported by Peel and the Conservatives against the Radicals. On balance, however, the cohesiveness of the Whig–Liberal–Radical combination tended to increase rather than to diminish. The gains made by the Conservatives in the general elections of 1835 and 1837 meant that the Whigs and their allies had to work more closely together in parliament if there was to be Whig rather than Conservative government; and although the bloc of Liberals which lay between the Whigs and the Philosophic Radicals sometimes voted with the latter against the former, they were not prepared to do so if it involved endangering the ministry. Grote and his colleagues, able though they were, did not have the weight and practical experience to offer a credible alternative to the Whigs as political leaders, and they were never able to win the general confidence of Liberal MPs or, more widely, of the newly enfranchised middle classes. Utilitarian ideas did have an appeal for progressive intellectuals, and in diluted form they had a significant influence on the mental climate of the time. But the Philosophic Radicals were not much concerned about some of the issues – especially those with a religious or denominational aspect – which were of major interest to the new electorate. For much of the 1830s, politically-minded Dissenters in the provinces tended to channel their energies into local affairs: Richard Cobden, for instance, was heavily involved in the campaign which led to the incorporation of Manchester in 1838 and the establishment of Liberal/Radical control at the first municipal elections. Subsequently, when men of this type broadened their horizons and began to play a larger part in national politics, they were able to operate from a much firmer base in provincial public opinion than the Philosophic Radicals had ever enjoyed.

Working-Class Perspectives on Post-Reform Politics

We have seen that there were differences between Whigs and Philosophic Radicals after 1832, especially concerning the desirability of further political reform. Over a number of other issues, however, there was relatively little disagreement between them. With regard to the major legislation of 1833–5, for example, the Utilitarians not only gave general support to the government but could also claim some of the credit for the measures concerned, notably on account of the important role played by Chadwick in the creation of the Factory Act of 1833 and the New Poor Law of 1834. Furthermore, such differences as there were between Whigs and Philosophic Radicals now seem rather insignificant compared with the gulf which separated the whole – or virtually the whole – spectrum of parliamentary opinion from working-class radicalism. The number of MPs who could be regarded as accredited spokesmen of the working classes was hardly greater after 1832 than it had been before. At the first general election after the Reform Act, Hunt lost his seat at Preston, and the joint success of William Cobbett and John Fielden (a manufacturer who advocated factory reform and universal suffrage) at Oldham was very untypical. Within months of the passing of the Act, Hunt's interpretation of it had come to be generally accepted in working-class circles. Resentment was directed against the Whigs who had devised the 'Humbug Bill', and against the middle-class reformers who had campaigned for it so strongly, and these resentments were heightened by the behaviour of both groups in the post-1832 period.

Although the Whigs' legislative record (at least in the first half of the decade) could be interpreted from one point of view as progressive, from another point of view the policies of the Grey and Melbourne governments could be seen as displaying a consistent indifference or even hostility to the interests of working men. The succession of episodes which created this impression had begun before the Reform Bill was passed or even introduced, when Lord Melbourne as Home Secretary showed considerable severity in suppressing the Swing riots. Soon afterwards the first prosecutions were brought against radical journalists and others for publishing or distributing unstamped periodicals; and the sustained effort made by the authorities over the next five years to enforce the duty imposed in 1819 – an effort which involved spells of imprisonment for nearly a thousand people – was interpreted as showing, in the words of an unstamped paper of 1833, 'the deadly hatred this treacherous Whig oligarchy feel towards the *Working Man's Press*'. (Wiener, 1969, p. 130.) Of the measures passed after the Reform Act, the one that did most to excite popular feeling was undoubtedly the Poor Law Amendment Act. Those who framed it wished to deter people from applying for assistance from the rates by restricting the practice of outdoor relief and making it necessary for those who wanted relief to enter a workhouse, where a harsh regime would be imposed on them. This policy was regarded by working people as a thoroughly heartless attack on the comfort, dignity and customary rights of the poor; and it was also interpreted by some as an attempt, by a parliament representing employers of labour, to induce workers to accept low wages as the only alternative to the workhouse. When the administrative machinery of the new system was being set up it provoked a very strong and sometimes violent protest movement, especially in the textile districts of Yorkshire and Lancashire; and in 1838 the reformed parliament's lack of sympathy with the lower classes was strikingly underlined by the fact that when Fielden organized a large-scale petitioning movement against the act of 1834 and introduced a motion for its repeal, the motion was defeated by 309 votes to 17.

A further aspect of what seemed to be a kind of *offensive* against the working classes and their means of self-protection was the action taken against trade unions. Particular indignation was aroused by the transportation of two groups of trade unionists, the 'Tolpuddle Martyrs' of 1834 and the leaders of the Glasgow spinners' strike of 1837, in spite of many demonstrations and petitions against the severity of the sentences passed on them. Finally, one should mention two other issues over which the Whig government and the reformed parliament were thought to have been, if not actively oppressive, at least unfeelingly deaf to the claims of working men. In the field of factory reform, Althorp's Act of 1833 was a severe disappointment to the 'short-time' movement, as it restricted the working hours of children in such a way that the hours of adult workers were not affected, and the ulterior purpose of the factory movement was thereby frustrated. 'What have we had since the Whigs passed the Reform Bill?' asked a Yorkshire operative at a public meeting in August 1833. 'We have had nothing but cruelty and hypocrisy, and this is a sample of the Liberty-loving Whigs.' (Ward, 1962, p. 111.) The second issue was the condition of the handloom weavers. There were still very large numbers of them in the 1830s, and their distress, resulting from underemployment and very low piece-rates, was more desperate than ever. Various remedies were suggested, such as the fixing of minimum wages (which had been proposed at intervals since the turn of the century) and the placing of restrictions or taxes on machinery. Investigations of the problem were carried out by a Commons select committee appointed in 1834 and a royal commission appointed three years later, and attempts to secure legislation were made in 1835–7 by MPs sympathetic to the weavers such as Fielden and John Maxwell, member for Lanarkshire. But strong opposition to state intervention was expressed by the devotees of political economy, headed by Charles Poulett Thomson, MP for Manchester and Vice-President of the Board of Trade, and proposals for legislation were decisively voted down.

Besides the nature of government policies, one of the principal causes of popular alienation from the reformed political system was the fact that very few MPs were willing to press for the measures of reform, political and social, which the working classes actually wanted. There were some philanthropists and social reformers who were distrustful of political economy and willing to vote against the New Poor Law and in favour of legislative protection for handloom weavers and factory workers; but very few of them were also thoroughgoing democrats. On the other hand, there were some MPs whose views on political reform were quite advanced, but whose views on social and economic issues aroused antagonism. Daniel O'Connell, who had led the movement for Catholic Emancipation, was a conspicuous example. He was prepared to support manhood suffrage, but in 1836 he voted for an attempt by Poulett Thomson to amend Althorp's Act by removing the restriction on the working hours of children over twelve, and in 1837 he expressed strong hostility to trade unions. He retained a large and loyal following in Ireland, but many Irishmen in England deserted him to follow the Chartist leader Feargus O'Connor, and he came to be regarded by the English working classes as a traitor.

Other political reformers who aroused popular distrust were the Philosophic Radicals. So far as 'organic' reform was concerned, the measure on which they laid most emphasis – as James Mill had earlier – was the ballot. They maintained that without it extensions of the electorate merely increased the number of voters subject to aristocratic influence and coercion, and Grote introduced motions for the ballot in every year but one between 1833 and 1839. Popular radicals, however, did not give such high priority to this measure. Indeed they believed that if it was introduced without being accompanied by a large extension of the suffrage, it would damage working-class interests by depriving the unenfranchised of what opportunities they had for influencing the behaviour of electors; in particular, it would undermine the practice of 'exclusive dealing', whereby working men reserved their custom for shopkeepers who voted for popular candidates. As for universal suffrage, the Philosophic Radicals professed to be committed to it in principle, but they did not take the lead in campaigning for it. They tended to hold the view that it was currently impracticable because it was strongly opposed by the middle classes and because the working classes had not yet been properly prepared for it. Roebuck said in a speech of 30 July 1833: 'The people at present are far too ignorant to render themselves happy, even though they should possess supreme power tomorrow.'

The Utilitarians did call for a large extension of popular education: it was while introducing a motion for a state system of primary schools that Roebuck made the remark just quoted. But the superior tone in which they advocated educational reform, and the transparent way in which education was linked in their minds to the propagation of 'correct' ideas on political economy, were not calculated to commend their plans to working-class radicals. Roebuck said in the same speech that one of the most important results of a proper education of the people would be a thorough understanding on their part of what government could do and what it could not do to relieve their distresses: 'Let them once understand thoroughly their social condition, and we shall have no more unmeaning discontents.' In opposition to such arguments J.B. ('Bronterre') O'Brien, the outstanding journalist of the unstamped press, went so far as to say that 'the only knowledge which is of any service to the working people is that which makes them more dissatisfied'; and many popular radicals were of the opinion that state education was undesirable, at least until such time as the state itself was under the people's control. (Hollis, 1970, p. 20.) There were other social issues, such as the New Poor Law and the handloom weavers, over which the gap between Utilitarian and popular radicals was even wider. One should not assume that the Utilitarians were callously indifferent to the sufferings of the poor. They were genuinely convinced that the Old Poor Law had contributed to the *growth* of pauperism, by undermining the self-reliance of working people and encouraging them to produce more children than they could support; and they believed that an artificial attempt to halt the decline of handloom weaving would prolong the weavers' distress by retarding their transition to other occupations. Such opinions, however – sincere and well-meaning though they may have been – inevitably distanced them from the working classes.

A factor on the other side which was helping to widen the gap between middle-class radicalism and working-class movements was the continued diffusion, in the years immediately after the Reform Bill, of socialist and anti-capitalist ideas. Such ideas were disseminated in various forms, and were often unaccompanied (as in the 1820s) by a commitment to *political* reform. Robert Owen, for example, had no faith in political agitation and democracy. In the 1820s his principal hope had been that the successful implementation of his ideas in experimental communities would set a trend which would soon be generally followed; in the early 1830s, encourged by the initial success of several schemes for co-operative production and marketing and by the active involvement of some trade unions in such schemes, he believed that the best chance of securing general adoption of his ideas lay in an expansion of trade union organization and a transformation of its objectives. The extent of his influence over the trade union movement at this time, and over the Grand National Consolidated Trades Union in particular, should not be exaggerated. Many people doubted, in particular, his notion that industry could be transferred from a competitive regime to a co-operative one through a *peaceful* revolution, without conflict with the capitalists. The editors of the two main Owenite journals of 1833–4, James Morrison of the Birmingham *Pioneer* and J.E. Smith of the *Crisis*, thought that a confrontation would be unavoidable and favoured the use of a general strike to bring industry under the control of the producers. Despite such disagreements, however, there certainly was in these years a coming together of several phenomena: a recognition by trade unions of the need for greater solidarity and mutual support; an optimism about the potential of producers' co-operatives; and an almost millenarian vision – which Owen did much to inspire – of social regeneration and universal brotherhood. There was a widespread belief that some combination of general unionism and co-operative socialism offered the best way forward, and that this route might circumvent the existing political system and the problems involved in radically reforming it.

There were others who, though sympathetic to socialism, were dubious about this kind of strategy; and pre-eminent among these was O'Brien, who became editor of the *Poor Man's Guardian* in November 1832. On the one hand, he regarded the conflict between capital and labour as of basic importance, and criticized those who overstressed the purely political mechanisms of exploitation. He repeatedly maintained that traditional objects of radical hostility such as taxes were insignificant as causes of working-class poverty when compared with the profits of capitalists and middlemen, and he claimed that the most serious conflict of interest was not (as the Philosophic Radicals held) that between aristocracy and people but that between the 'profit-hunting classes' and the 'productive classes'. At the same time, however, he maintained that trade union or co-operative activity, however extensively organized, would be unable to succeed while the control of the state was in hostile hands, and that the exploitation of labour by capital, like other forms of exploitation, could only be ended by means of *political* change. Hodgskin had observed that ultimately it was the law of property and the control of the property-owning classes over the law which enabled those classes to appropriate the fruits of other men's labour, but he had not gone on to draw the conclusion that popular control of the legislature was essential. O'Brien did draw this conclusion, very insistently. Moreover, he had a distinct idea of the new social order – one involving public ownership of land and the transference of the control of industry from capitalists to producers – which could be brought into being by means of political democracy.

While socialist ideas – both of the Owenite brand and of O'Brien's democratic variety – were prominent in the unstamped press of the early 1830s, and many papers carried attacks on capitalist profits and political economy, these themes only partially displaced the older brand of radicalism whose main targets were taxation, corruption, the aristocracy and the Church. A number of writers, including Cobbett and Carlile, continued to focus on such topics, which were also played upon by middle-class radicals. Moreover, the collapse of the Grand National Consolidated Trades Union within months of its formation disappointed the many hopes that had been invested in it, and (together with the failure of several co-operative ventures) weakened the practical appeal of socialism in working-class circles. When the boom of the mid-thirties gave way to depression in 1837–8, and political agitation revived, the division between middle-class and working-class radicals was not so sharp as to preclude *all* collaboration between them. A few middle-class figures in London and Birmingham were involved in the drafting of the People's Charter and the National Petition, and the London Working Men's Association secured undertakings from a number of Radical MPs to support the six points. None the less the fact remains that in the period between 1832 and approximately the middle of the century, a deep distrust of the middle classes and an uncompromising insistence on the pursuit of specifically working-class objectives were the main features of popular agitation.

Conclusion

Class feeling was not new in the thirties and forties, but it was probably more widespread and entrenched than it had been previously. Earlier in the century a strong sense of working-class solidarity had been generated in some parts of the country through the post-war movement for universal suffrage, and antagonism had been felt not only towards aristocratic boroughmongers but also towards those *within* the reform movement who refused to press for the enfranchisement of working men. In the same decade antagonism towards employers had been evident in many situations of industrial conflict. On occasions the employers had been backed in one way or another by the state, and working men had found themselves confronted with both at once; this had happened, for instance, over the Luddite disturbances of 1811–12 and over the apprenticeship clauses of the Statute of Artificers in 1813–14. But in general, hostility towards employers had been somewhat distinct from hostility towards the political system and those who operated it, and antagonisms had been less focused than they became in the thirties and forties.

One reason why, in the latter decades, working-class resentments were consolidated to a greater extent into a broad sense of hostility towards the propertied and employing classes was the political settlement of 1832. Previously, in the political sphere, the conflict of interest with the middle classes had been more potential than real, and there had been some acceptance of the idea that the middle and working classes constituted together an excluded 'people' and had a shared interest in attacking aristocratic monopoly and privilege. After 1832, the line which separated the political nation from those outside it corresponded closely to the social dividing line between the propertied classes and the rest of the community. This dichotomy did a great deal – as Mackintosh had predicted in 1818 – to give the working classes a collective sense of grievance; and the feeling was strengthened, of course, by what was perceived as heavy class-bias in the legislation of the post-Reform Bill years. Furthermore, the notion that in social and economic relations there was a basic conflict of interest between capitalists and workers was more widely absorbed and articulated in the second quarter of the century than in the first. This was partly due to the ideological developments that have been mentioned; although few Chartists adopted the full logic of a socialist analysis, the popularization of anti-capitalist ideas stemming from the writings of Hodgskin, O'Brien and others helped to give working men in a variety of situations a sense of participating in a *general* struggle between capital and labour. But probably of more fundamental importance were changes in the structure of industry, and what seemed (especially in 1837–42) to be a growing instability in the economy. Not only the outworkers in textiles and artisans in the clothing trades who had provided the main body of support for radical movements in the Regency period, but also many other occupational groups – cotton spinners in Lancashire factories, for instance, and metalworkers in Birmingham – felt that their position in relation to their employers was weakening and that their security was threatened. One of the motives that drove unprecedentedly large numbers of people into radical politics was the hope that by obtaining control over legislation they could somehow check these adverse trends and alter the balance of power between labour and capital.

However, while Chartism was both a more comprehensive movement and a more strongly class-conscious one than the reform agitation of 1816–19, what in the last analysis is most striking about the two movements is how similar they were. Emerging from the flux and disruption of industrialization and demographic change, they were the high points of a phase of unusual militancy in working-class politics. They were both marked by the same insistence on universal suffrage, the same attempts to intimidate parliament through mass meetings and petitioning, and the same tendency to resort to conspiracy and insurrection when public agitation was frustrated. Also, they were both marked by failure. In 1829–32, a strategy of extra-parliamentary pressure did help to achieve a reform of parliament; but that campaign was different from those of the 1810s and the 1840s, involving as it did a wide range of social groups from working men to country gentlemen. The movements led by Henry Hunt in 1816–19 and by Feargus O'Connor in the late thirties and forties were both inspired by the belief that the working classes not only needed political power but could actually win it for themselves. By around the middle of the century, after the setbacks of 1839, 1842 and 1848, belief in this possibility had faded. At the same period, a falling off in the severity of cyclical depressions was taking some of the urgency out of popular demands for change, and several significant reforms of a social and economic nature (while themselves attributable in part to the alarms aroused by militant Chartism) weakened the case for regarding full democracy as the indispensable pre-requisite for an improvement in working-class conditions. The fulfilment of the political aims of Huntite and Chartist campaigners was to be a much more protracted process than they would have anticipated or thought acceptable; and the reforms that enfranchised working men in the late nineteenth and early twentieth centuries were to be achieved more by joint action with allies in other classes then through a full-blooded challenge to the existing order.

References and Further Reading

An asterisk indicates books particularly relevant for further reading.

Beer, Max 1929: *A History of British Socialism.* 2nd edn, 2 vols. London: Bell

Behagg, Clive 1982: An Alliance with the Middle Class: The Birmingham Political Union and Early Chartism. In James Epstein and Dorothy Thompson (eds), *The Chartist Experience: Studies in Working-Class Radicalism and Culture, 1830–1860,* London: Macmillan, 59–86

Belchem, John 1978: Henry Hunt and the Evolution of the Mass Platform. *English Historical Review*, 93, 739–73

Belchem, John 1981: Republicanism, Popular Constitutionalism and the Radical Platform in Early Nineteenth-Century England. *Social History*, 6, 1–32

*Belchem, John 1985: '*Orator*' Hunt: Henry Hunt and English Working-Class Radicalism. Oxford: Clarendon Press

Bohstedt, John 1983: *Riots and Community Politics in England and Wales 1790–1810.* Cambridge, Mass.: Harvard University Press

Briggs, Asa 1948: Thomas Attwood and the Economic Background of the Birmingham Political Union. *Cambridge Historical Journal*, 9, 190–216

Briggs, Asa 1952: The Background of the Parliamentary Reform Movement in Three English Cities (1830–2). *Cambridge Historical Journal*, 10, 293–317

*Brock, Michael 1973: *The Great Reform Act.* London: Hutchinson

Calhoun, Craig 1982: *The Question of Class Struggle: Social Foundations of Popular Radicalism during the Industrial Revolution.* Oxford: Blackwell

*Cannon, John 1973: *Parliamentary Reform 1640–1832.* Cambridge: Cambridge University Press

Claeys, Gregory 1983: The Triumph of Class-Conscious Reformism in British Radicalism, 1790–1860. *Historical Journal*, 26, 969–85.

Clark, J. C. D. 1985: *English Society 1688–1832: Ideology, Social Structure and Political Practice during the Ancien Regime.* Cambridge: Cambridge University Press

Collini, Stefan, Winch, Donald and Burrow, John 1983: *That Noble Science of Politics: A Study in Nineteenth-Century Intellectual History.* Cambridge: Cambridge University Press

Cookson, J. E. 1982: *The Friends of Peace: Anti-War Liberalism in England 1793–1815*. Cambridge: Cambridge University Press

Dickinson, H. T. 1985: *British Radicalism and the French Revolution 1789–1815*. Oxford: Blackwell. Historical Association Studies

Dinwiddy, J. R. 1971: *Christopher Wyvill and Reform 1790–1820*. York: Borthwick Institute of Historical Research. Borthwick Papers No. 39

Dinwiddy, J. R. 1978: The Classical Economists and the Utilitarians. In E. K. Bramsted and K. J. Melhuish (eds), *Western Liberalism*, London: Longman, 12–25

Dinwiddy, J. R. 1979: Luddism and Politics in the Northern Counties. *Social History*, 4, 33–63

Dinwiddy, J. R. 1980: Sir Francis Burdett and Burdettite Radicalism. *History*, 65, 17–31

Dinwiddy, J. R. 1985: The 'Influence of the Crown' in the Early Nineteenth Century: A Note on the Opposition Case. *Parliamentary History*, 4, 189–200

Donnelly, F. K. and Baxter, J. L. 1975. Sheffield and the English Revolutionary Tradition 1791–1820. *International Review of Social History*, 20, 398–423

Evans, E. J. 1983: *The Forging of the Modern State: Early Industrial Britain 1783–1870*. London: Longman

Ferguson, Henry 1960: The Birmingham Political Union and the Government 1831–32. *Victorian Studies*, 3, 261–76

Flick, Carlos 1978: *The Birmingham Political Union and the Movements for Reform in Britain 1830–1839*. Folkestone: Dawson

Gash, Norman 1953: *Politics in the Age of Peel: A Study in the Technique of Parliamentary Representation 1830–1850*. London: Longman

Glen, Robert 1984: *Urban Workers in the Early Industrial Revolution*. London: Croom Helm

Halévy, Elie 1956: *Thomas Hodgskin*. Translated by A. J. Taylor. London: Benn

Hamburger, Joseph 1962: James Mill on Universal Suffrage and the Middle Class. *Journal of Politics*, 24, 167–90

Hamburger, Joseph 1963: *James Mill and the Art of Revolution*. New Haven, Conn.: Yale University Press

Hamburger, Joseph 1965: *Intellectuals in Politics: John Stuart Mill and the Philosophic Radicals*. New Haven, Conn.: Yale University Press

Hammond, J. L. and Hammond, B. 1919: *The Skilled Labourer 1760–1832*. London: Longman

Harrison, J. F. C. 1969: *Robert Owen and the Owenites in Britain and America*. London: Routledge & Kegan Paul

Hendrix, Richard 1976: Popular Humor and 'The Black Dwarf'. *Journal of British Studies*, 16, 108–28

Himmelfarb, Gertrude 1984: *The Idea of Poverty: England in the Early Industrial Age*. London: Faber & Faber

Hollis, Patricia 1970: *The Pauper Press: A Study in Working-Class Radicalism of the 1830s*. Oxford: Oxford University Press

Hone, J. Ann 1982: *For the Cause of Truth: Radicalism in London 1796-1821.* Oxford: Clarendon Press

Johnson, Richard 1979: 'Really Useful Knowledge': Radical Education and Working-Class Culture, 1790-1848. In John Clarke, Chas Critcher and Richard Johnson (eds), *Working-Class Culture: Studies in History and Theory*, London: Hutchinson, 75-102

Jones, Gareth Stedman 1983: *Languages of Class: Studies in English Working Class History 1832-1982.* Cambridge: Cambridge University Press

Kaijage, F. J. 1976: Working-Class Radicalism in Barnsley, 1816-1820. In Sidney Pollard and Colin Holmes (eds), *Essays in the Economic and Social History of South Yorkshire*, Sheffield: South Yorkshire County Council, 118-34

Kinzer, B. L. 1982. *The Ballot Question in Nineteenth-Century British Politics.* New York: Garland

Kirby, R. G. and Musson, A. E. 1975: *The Voice of the People: John Doherty, 1798-1854, Trade Unionist, Radical and Factory Reformer.* Manchester: Manchester University Press

Kriegel, A. D. 1980: Liberty and Whiggery in Early Nineteenth Century England. *Journal of Modern History*, 52, 253-78

Lee, Janice 1982: Political Antiquarianism Unmasked: The Conservative Attack on the Myth of the Ancient Constitution. *Bulletin of the Institute of Historical Research*, 55, 166-79

McCord, Norman 1967: Some Difficulties of Parliamentary Reform. *Historical Journal*, 10, 376-90

Milton-Smith, John 1972: Earl Grey's Cabinet and the Objects of Parliamentary Reform. *Historical Journal*, 15, 55-74

Mitchell, Austin 1965: The Whigs and Parliamentary Reform to 1830. *Historical Studies (Australia and New Zealand)*, 12, 22-42

Mitchell, Austin 1967: *The Whigs in Opposition 1815-30.* Oxford: Clarendon Press

Mitchell, Leslie 1980: *Holland House.* London: Duckworth

Moore, D. C. 1966: Concession or Cure: The Sociological Premises of the First Reform Act. *Historical Journal*, 9, 39-59

Moore, D. C. 1976: *The Politics of Deference.* Brighton: Harvester Press

Morris, R. J. 1979: *Class and Class Consciousness in the Industrial Revolution 1780-1850.* London: Macmillan

New, Chester 1961: *The Life of Henry Brougham to 1830.* Oxford: Clarendon Press

Oliver, W. H. 1954: Organisations and Ideas behind the Efforts to achieve a General Union of the Working Classes in the Early 1830s. Unpublished D.Phil. thesis, University of Oxford

Osborne, J. W. 1972: *John Cartwright.* Cambridge: Cambridge University Press

Parssinen, T. M. 1972: The Revolutionary Party in London, 1816-20. *Bulletin of the Institute of Historical Research*, 45, 266-82

*Prothero, Iorwerth 1979: *Artisans and Politics in Early Nineteenth-Century London: John Gast and His Times.* Folkestone: Dawson

83

Read, Donald 1958: *Peterloo: The 'Massacre' and its Background*. Manchester: Manchester University Press

Read, Donald 1961: *Press and People 1790–1850: Opinion in Three English Cities*. London: Edward Arnold

Richards, Paul 1980: State Formation and Class Struggle, 1832–48. In Philip Corrigan (ed.), *Capitalism, State Formation and Marxist Theory*, London: Quartet Books, 49–78

Rowe, D. J. 1977: London Radicalism in the Era of the Great Reform Bill. In John Stevenson (ed.), *London in the Age of Reform*, Oxford: Blackwell, 149–76

*Royle, Edward and Walvin, James 1982: *English Radicals and Reformers 1760–1848*. Brighton: Harvester Press

Rubinstein, William 1983: The End of 'Old Corruption' in Britain 1780–1860. *Past and Present*, 101, 55–86

Smith, E. A. 1975: *Whig Principles and Party Politics: Earl Fitzwilliam and the Whig Party, 1748–1833*. Manchester: Manchester University Press

Spater, George 1982: *William Cobbett: The Poor Man's Friend*. 2 vols. Cambridge: Cambridge University Press

Stevenson, John (ed.) 1977: *London in the Age of Reform*. Oxford: Blackwell

Sykes, R. A. 1980: Some Aspects of Working-Class Consciousness in Oldham, 1830–1842. *Historical Journal*, 23, 167–79

Sykes, R. A. 1982: Popular Politics and Trade Unionism in South-East Lancashire, 1829–42. Unpublished Ph.D. thesis, University of Manchester

Thomas, William 1962: Francis Place and Working Class History. *Historical Journal*, 5, 61–70

Thomas, William 1969: James Mill's Politics: The 'Essay on Government' and the Movement for Reform. *Historical Journal*, 12, 249–84

Thomas, William 1979: *The Philosophic Radicals: Nine Studies in Theory and Practice 1817–1841*. Oxford: Clarendon Press

Thomis, M. I. and Holt, P. 1977: *Threats of Revolution in Britain 1789–1848*. London: Macmillan

*Thompson, E. P. 1968: *The Making of the English Working Class*. 2nd edn. Harmondsworth: Penguin

Thompson, N. W. 1984: *The People's Science: The Popular Political Economy of Exploitation and Crisis 1816–34*. Cambridge: Cambridge University Press

Wallas, Graham 1925: *The Life of Francis Place 1771–1854*. 4th edn. London: Allen & Unwin

Ward, J. T. 1962: *The Factory Movement, 1830–1855*. London: Macmillan

Wasson, E. A. 1980: The Spirit of Reform, 1832 and 1867. *Albion*, 12, 164–74

Wasson, E. A. 1985: The Great Whigs and Parliamentary Reform 1809–1830. *Journal of British Studies*, 24, 434–64

Wickwar, W. H. 1928: *The Struggle for the Freedom of the Press 1819–1832.* London: Allen & Unwin

Wiener, J. H. 1969: *The War of the Unstamped: The Movement to Repeal the British Newspaper Tax, 1830–1836.* Ithaca, NY: Cornell University Press

Wiener, J. H. 1983: *Radicalism and Freethought in Nineteenth-Century Britain: The Life of Richard Carlile.* Westport, Conn.: Greenwood Press

Woolley, S. F. 1938: The Personnel of the Parliament of 1833. *English Historical Review*, 53, 240–62

Index

Allen, John, 4
Althorp, Viscount, 9, 50–3, 60, 68–9
America, United States of, 11, 57–8
Anglo-Saxon constitution, 31, 40
annual parliaments, 14, 25, 57, 62
anti-capitalism, 40–4, 63–4, 76–7, 79
apprenticeship, 23, 26, 28, 78
Argus, The, 13
arming, 22, 34
Ashton-under-Lyne, 66
Attwood, Thomas, 11, 46, 56–7, 54–5, 70

Bacon, Thomas, 36
Baines, Edward, 11–12, 66
ballot, 49, 57, 59, 62, 69–70, 74–5
Bamford, Samuel, 24, 25, 38
Barnsley, 36
Benbow, William, 67
Bennet, H. G., 4, 12, 35
Bentham, Jeremy, 14–18, 31–2, 43, 57–8, 70
Benthamites, 14–18, 43, 57–60, 70–2, 74–5
Birmingham, 11, 12–13, 33, 45, 48, 64–5, 77, 79
Birmingham Political Union, 45–6, 54–6, 60, 64–5, 70
Black Dwarf, 31, 37
Blandford, Marquess of, 45
Bolton Chronicle, 43
boroughs, small (decayed/pocket/rotten), 6, 8, 9, 45, 47, 51, 67, 68
Brand, Thomas, 6
Brandreth, Jeremiah, 35
Briggs, Asa, 65
Bristol riots, 46, 54, 67
British Association for Promoting Co-operative Knowledge, 62
Brotherton, Joseph, 70
Brougham, Henry, Lord, 2, 3, 4, 12, 51
Buller, Charles, 58–9, 70
Burdett, Sir Francis, 5, 19–21, 28, 31, 34, 38, 55

Cambridge, 15
Canning, George, 49
Canningites, 45, 46
Cap of Liberty, 37
Carlile, Richard, 30, 34, 38–40, 62, 77
Caroline of Brunswick, Queen, 8, 9, 37–8
Carpenter, William, 62–3
Cartwright, John, 19–21, 23–5, 30–2, 40
Catholic Emancipation, 4, 10, 45, 50, 56

Cato Street Conspiracy, 34
Chadwick, Edwin, 70, 72
Chandos, Marquess of, 49
Chartism, 77, 79–80
Cheshire, 26
Church of England, 16, 17, 39, 77
clothworkers, 22, 66
Cobbett, William, 20, 24, 25, 28–31, 37, 39, 40–1, 44, 56, 62, 63, 72, 77
Cobbett's Political Register, 24, 28, 37, 39
Cobden, Richard, 71
combination laws, 26, 43–4
Conservatives, 1, 68, 71
co-operative movement, 41, 44, 61, 62, 76
Corn Laws, 1, 12, 13–14, 57
corruption, 8, 16–17, 21, 29, 30, 52, 67, 68, 70, 77
cotton industry, 21–2, 27, 56–7, 61; *see also* weavers, handloom, *and* spinners, cotton
country gentlemen, 3, 9–10, 19, 48, 79
county association movement, 10, 48
county MPs, 12, 48, 51
Coventry, 65
Crisis, The, 76
Croker, J. W., 49
Crown, Influence of the, 2–4
currency, 40–1, 56–7, 64

Democratic Recorder, 37
Derbyshire, 35, 36
Devonshire, 6th Duke of, 9
Dickinson, H. T., 19
Disraeli, Benjamin, 50
Dissenters, 11–13, 50, 57, 69–71
Doherty, John, 61
Durham, Earl of, *see* Lambton, J. G.

East Anglia, 26
East Retford, 12, 45
economic depression, 20, 24, 27, 28, 41, 44, 45, 56, 77, 80
economical reform, 3, 6
Edinburgh Review, 2, 3, 5–8, 17, 20, 57
Edmonds, George, 64
education, 4, 17, 75
evangelicalism, 39–40, 69

Factory Act of 1833, 69, 72–4
factory movement, 61, 66, 72, 73
Fielden, John, 72–4
Fitzwilliam, 2nd Earl, 5, 9
Fox, Charles James, 1
framework-knitters, 22, 28, 36, 43
free thought, 39, 62

French Revolution, 2, 19, 26, 30
French Revolution of 1830, 46, 51, 55

general strike, 67, 76
George III, 1, 3
George IV, previously Prince of Wales
  and Prince Regent, 2, 8, 33, 37–8, 46
Giant-Killer, The, 29
Glasgow, 73
Gorgon, The, 32
Grafton, 4th Duke of, 9
Grampound, 8, 12
Grand National Consolidated Trades
  Union, 76, 77
Grange Moor rising, 35
Great Northern Union, 39, 40
Grenville Whigs, 5, 6
Greville, Charles, 49–50
Grey, 2nd Earl, 5, 6, 8, 46, 47, 49–51,
  56, 68, 72
Grote, George, 58, 70, 71, 74

Halifax, 24
Hamburger, Joseph, 59
Hammond, J. L. and B., 35
Hampden Clubs, 10, 25, 27, 34
hatters, 26
Henson, Gravener, 28, 43
Hetherington, Henry, 62–4
Hobhouse, Sir John Cam, 35, 50, 55, 60
Hodgskin, Thomas, 41–4, 64, 77, 79
Holland, 3rd Lord, 5–8, 51
Hone, William, 37
hosiery trade, 22, 28, 61; *see also*
  framework-knitters
Huddersfield, 35
Hume, Joseph, 3, 44, 70
Hunt, Henry, 19, 25, 28–30, 34, 37–40,
  44, 62–3, 66, 67, 72, 79

Irishmen, 20, 22, 62, 68, 74

Jeffrey, Francis, 5–6, 52

Knight, John, 23, 24, 38

labour theory of value, 30, 41, 42
Lambton, J. G., 1st Earl of Durham, 2,
  8, 49, 53, 60
Lancashire, 21–5, 27, 30, 33, 66, 73, 79
landownership, 7, 16–17, 29–30, 36; *see
  also* Spenceans
law reform, 4, 14, 16, 58, 69
Leeds, 11, 12, 18, 48, 65–6
Leeds Mercury, 11–12, 66
Leicestershire, 25–6
Liberals, 68, 70, 71
Liverpool, 11
Liverpool, 2nd Earl of, 1, 3, 4, 45
London, 6, 25, 26, 27, 28, 36, 37, 38,
  60, 62, 66, 77
London Corresponding Society, 19, 28
London Working Men's Association, 77
Londonderry, 2nd Marquess of, previously

Viscount Castlereagh, 3
Lords, House of, 9, 12, 46, 54, 59, 60,
  66
Luddism, 10, 21–2, 24, 25, 78; *see also*
  machinery

Macaulay, T. B., 57–8
machinery, 22, 27, 41, 65–6, 73; *see also*
  Luddism
Mackintosh, Sir James, 4, 6–8, 52, 78
Malthus, T. R., 13, 29, 43–4
Manchester, 12, 22–4, 33, 38, 48, 65–7,
  71
Manchester Courier, 56
Manchester Gazette, 18
Manchester Guardian, 12, 65
Manchester Political Union, 66
Manchester Times, 61
Marshall, John, 12, 18
Maxwell, John, 74
mass meetings, 25, 33, 37, 79
Medusa, The, 37
Melbourne, 2nd Viscount, 69, 72
Mellor, George, 35
metal trades, 65, 79
Methodism, 39–40
Middleton, 22, 25, 30, 66
Mill, James, 14–15, 17, 43, 57–9, 70, 74
Mill, John Stuart, 70
Milton, Viscount, 9, 12
minimum-wage regulations, 22, 28, 43, 73
Molesworth, Sir William, 70
monarchy, 16, 40, 51, 69
Moore, D. C., 51–2
Morning Chronicle, 15
Morrison, James, 76
Municipal Corporations Act, 69

National Association for the Protection of
  Labour, 61
National Debt, 29, 36, 56
National Political Union, 60
National Union of the Working Classes,
  61–2, 64, 66, 67
Newcastle, 4th Duke of, 67
Newcastle upon Tyne, 29
New Poor Law, 69, 72–5
Northmore, Thomas, 10
Norwich, 19
Nottingham, 34, 67
Nottingham Review, 21
Nottinghamshire, 25–6

Oastler, Richard, 61, 66
O'Brien, J. B. ('Bronterre'), 75–7, 79
O'Connell, Daniel, 45, 68, 74
O'Connor, Feargus, 74, 79
Oldham, 72
Oliver, William, 34
Orders in Council, 11, 12
Owen, Robert, 41, 43, 61, 76

Paine, Thomas, 19, 26, 32, 39
Parkes, Joseph, 59–60

Parliamentary History and Review, 17, 18
patronage, 3, 8, 46, 47
peace movement, 11, 23
Peel, Sir Robert, 4, 69, 71
Penryn, 12
Pentrich rising, 35, 36
Peterloo, 8, 9, 12, 33, 34, 37
petitioning, 11, 12, 24, 25, 27, 33, 53, 56, 73, 79
Philosophic Radicals, 70–1, 74–5, 77
Pioneer, The, 76
Pitt, William, 3, 5
Pittites, 2, 4
Place, Francis, 28, 32–3, 35, 43–4, 53, 59–60, 70
placemen, 3–4, 21, 45
political economy, 2, 13–14, 43–4, 65, 75, 77
Political Protestants, 34
Political Union of the Working Classes (Manchester), 66, 67
Poor Law Amendment Act, *see* New Poor Law
Poor Man's Advocate, 61
Poor Man's Guardian, 63–4, 76
population growth, 13, 26, 28–9, 75
Portland, 3rd Duke of, 5
potteries, Staffordshire, 11, 61
Prentice, Archibald, 18, 61, 66
Preston, 62, 72

Radical Reform Association, 62
repression, 9, 19, 21, 3, 35
Republican, The, 37
republicanism, 39–40
revolution, threats of, 21–2, 34–7, 50–1, 54, 59–60
Rhodes, Ebenezer, 11
Ricardo, David, 13–14, 58
Richmond, 3rd Duke of, 19
rights, historic, 31–4
rights, natural, 30, 32, 42
rights of labour, 30–1, 42
riots, 24, 26; *see also* Bristol riots, Luddism, Swing riots
Rockinghamite Whigs, 2–3
Roebuck, J. A., 70, 75
Romilly, Sir Samuel, 2, 4
Roscoe, William, 11
Rubinstein, William, 4
Russell, Lord John, 8–9, 12, 38, 46, 47, 52–3, 69–70

Scholefield, Joshua, 70
Scotland, 2, 34, 47
Sheffield, 11, 19, 34, 48, 65
Sheffield Independent, 18
Sherwin, William, 30
Sherwin's Political Register, 30, 32, 34, 37
Sidmouth, Viscount, 24
Six Acts (1819), 9, 38
slavery, abolition of, 69
Smith, Sydney, 17
socialism, 40–4, 58, 76–7, 79

Society of the Friends of the People, 47
Spa Fields, London, 25, 33
Spence, Thomas, 29
Spenceans, 29–30, 36, 40, 62
spies, 34, 36
spinners, cotton, 61, 65, 73, 79
Spooner, Richard, 11
Statute of Artificers, 23, 28, 78
Stockport, 27, 40
suffrage, household, 11, 15, 25
suffrage, universal, 7, 9, 15, 20, 25, 30–2, 57, 62, 63, 66, 72, 75, 78, 79
suffrage, women's, 15
Swing riots, 46, 51, 72

taxation, 3, 20–1, 25, 28, 40, 56, 58, 63
Taylor, John Edward, 12
Test and Corporation Acts, repeal of, 69
Thistlewood, Arthur, 29, 34, 36, 37
Thompson, E. P., 35–6
Thompson, William, 44
Thomson, Charles Poulett, 74
Tolpuddle Martyrs, 73
Tories, 13, 45, 49–50, 54, 56, 68, 69, 71
Trades' Newspaper, 43
trade unions, 26, 27, 43–4, 61, 73, 74, 76, 77

Ultra-Tories, 45, 46, 56
underground politics, 20, 22, 34–6, 79
Unitarians, 11–12, 17–18
unstamped press, 63, 72, 75, 77
Utilitarians, *see* Benthamites

Voice of the People, 61

Wade, John, 32
Waithman, Robert, 6
Wales, 47
Ward, T. A., 18
wars, French, 3, 11. 19–21, 24, 26
Watson, James, 29, 37
weavers, handloom, 22–3, 27, 65–6, 73–4, 75
weavers, linen, 36
Wedgwood, Josiah, 11
Wellington, 1st Duke of, 4, 45, 46, 51. 60
Westminster, 20–1, 28
Westminster Review, 17, 57
Wetherell, Sir Charles, 67
Whigs (Foxite), 1–10, 12, 20, 38, 45–60, 63, 67, 68–73
Whitbread, Samuel, 6
Wilbraham, Bootle, 38
William, IV, 46, 50, 51, 54
Wood, G. W., 70
Wooler, T. J., 31–2, 38
woollen industry, 21; *see also* clothworkers
Wyvill, Christopher, 20, 48

Yorkshire, 12, 21–2, 73

Zetetic Societies, 40

Printed in the United Kingdom
by Lightning Source UK Ltd.
134247UK00001B/160-183/P